A FAMILY OF

Faith

Catechesis for the Whole Family

PARENT'S GUIDE

VOLUME II: THE SACRAMENTS

SOPHIA
INSTITUTE PRESS

Based on a program conceived by
Mary Mosher

Authors
Veronica Burchard
Jackie Diebold
Sean Fitzpatrick
Jose Gonzalez
Michael Gutzwiller
Karen Hettrick
John LaBarbara
Anna Maria Mendell
Mary Mosher

Editors
Veronica Burchard
Carolyn McKinney
Anna Maria Mendell

Academic Advisor
Douglas Bushman, S.T.L.
Michel Therrien, S.T.L., S.T.D.

Special Thanks
Terry Bolduc
Suzanne Walsh

Illustrator
Mary MacArthur

Mary Mosher, catechist, founder of Holy Family Academy in Manchester, NH, and mother of five adult children who are practicing Catholics, developed and continually refined a version of this program for 24 years at Ste. Marie Parish in Manchester, NH. Mary has a Master of Arts in Theology and Christian Ministry from the Franciscan University of Steubenville with a concentration in catechetics and additionally is certified in catechetics from the Franciscan University. We could not be more grateful to Mary for her help and advice, her service to the Church, and her efforts to lead souls closer to Christ.

This supplemental resource is not eligible for review by the USCCB. It has been reviewed for doctrinal soundness by our academic and theological advisors.

Cover Image
Icon of the Holy Family of Nazareth, inspired by Peter Murphy, written by Fabrizio Diomedi, © Peter Murphy and Fabrizio Diomedi. Photograph © Joe Gavin, Frank Gavin Photography.

Printed in the United States of America
Design by Perceptions Design Studio

A Family of Faith: Catechesis for the Whole Family Parent's Guide
Volume II: The Sacraments
ISBN: 978-1-622824-861

CONTENTS

QUICK START GUIDE

Follow the steps below to get the most out of *A Family of Faith*.

STEP 1: Read the "getting started" information in September and do the activities.

STEP 2: Before teaching each month, read the "what you need to know" sections in each activity. Make notes as you read and underline or highlight words to help you think through the content.

STEP 3: Do the activities with your children.

STEP 4: Look for simple ways to integrate discussions into the rhythms of your family life. Read saint stories at bedtime, talk about some of the topics in the car, while waiting in line at the store, or over dinner.

STEP 5: Reevaluate each month. Space is provided for you to make notes about what went well and what didn't. Remember that you can change your approach at any time!

A note on age-level suggestions

Every child is different. Take into account each child's reading ability as well as his or her maturity level when deciding which activities and "words to know" you will do. In this guide, activities are marked with a suggested age level. Feel free to ignore these suggestions and do the activities that work best for your children.

MAKING THE MOST OF ACTIVITIES

We know from Jesus, our Master Teacher, that true learning takes place in a setting of love. St. John Bosco, patron of teachers, said, "It is not enough to love the children; they have to know that they are loved." You're their parent: you've got this!

Here are some tips for turning even the simplest learning activities into worthwhile formative experiences, through your parental love.

Get more out of coloring

Coloring pages provide children with an opportunity to learn some basic facts and make connections. While your children are coloring a picture, ask them about specific details in it. For example: Why is Mary Magdelene kneeling before Jesus? Why are they throwing stones at St. Stephen? What do you see above the heads of the Apostles in the drawing of the Holy Spirit's descent at Pentecost?

Get more out of drawing

Young children who cannot write well can demonstrate their thought processes through drawing. As your children are drawing, ask them to explain their choices. Ask about colors, size, facial expressions, and any and all details.

Get more out of writing

Writing is an opportunity for your children to reflect on their thinking and become more aware of their thought processes. Ask your children to read their written responses aloud, and talk with them about what they wrote. Ask them about their favorite part of a story or to explain how they came to a certain conclusion. Never use writing as a threat or as a punishment.

Get more out of discussion

When asking questions, always start with those that are easy to answer before moving to more difficult ones. This helps "prime the pump." Admit when you don't know something, and express enthusiasm about figuring out the answer together. If you approach learning as an adventure, your children will, too!

More resources for children

Sign up for monthly eLessons at **SophiaInstituteforTeachers.org**:

- **Heavenly Hall of Fame:** Get two new saint biographies, activities, and coloring pages each month.
- **Joy of the Gospel** and **Teaching the Faith with Current Events:** Get an activity for all of the Sunday Gospel readings each month and a monthly discussion guide on current events.

September
GETTING STARTED

In every way, the Sacraments are about God's love, fully revealed in Jesus Christ. The seven Sacraments—the foundation of Christian living—will be the focus of our study this year. We will learn about each of the Sacraments: Baptism, Confirmation, Eucharist, Penance and Reconciliation, Anointing of the Sick, Holy Orders, and Matrimony.

The Sacraments are important parts of each stage of life, in which we receive God's free gift of grace. Through the grace given to us in the Sacraments, Jesus brings us into communion with Himself, the Father, and the Holy Spirit, and with one another in the Church.

As we begin our learning this year, let us rejoice that Jesus is here with us in the Sacraments!

YOUR CHILD'S FIRST TEACHER

Who is your children's first teacher? Who is your children's most important teacher? You are! Despite what our culture often tries to tell us, being a teacher does NOT require any special skills or certifications for parents. We are always teaching our children! We are teaching them even when we are not trying.

Teaching is what we do naturally, just as learning from parents is what children do naturally. In *Quality Education is Not Rocket Science*, Catholic educator Anthony Esolen writes, "Do not be afraid. ...This is not quantum physics. Children learn naturally, and if they are treated well, they will learn most things with ease." Especially in the younger years, before peer groups become more influential, parental guidance is far and away the most important factor in who a child grows up to be. And even once kids enter their teen years, parents continue to have more influence than they may think.

Over the next nine months, this program will give you all the knowledge and tools you need to educate your children in the Catholic Faith, and specifically the *Catechism of the Catholic Church*.

As you all grow in your faith together, your children will be learning not just from the fun activities they do, but even more from your example and witness. This is something they cannot get in any classroom, no matter how good that classroom is.

Read and reflect on the quotation below. Then spend a few minutes thinking or discussing with your spouse ways you can teach your children the Faith that don't involve creating a "classroom" type setting.

"The ministry of evangelization carried out by Christian parents is original and irreplaceable. It assumes the characteristics typical of family life itself, which should be interwoven with love, simplicity, practicality and daily witness."

–FAMILIARIS CONSORTIO

YOUR GRACE PEOPLE

Out of all of God's creatures, only human beings are created in the image and likeness of God. We are the only ones who can know and love our creator! And we are the only ones who can receive the Sacraments—signs instituted by Christ that give us His grace.

This year, use the template provided on **Grace Person Template (page 20 in the children's activity book)** to create a representation of each person in your family. Each month, a "Grace Person" activity will guide you to decorate or create symbols of the grace we receive, and place them on your grace people.

Be creative in where you display them in your home throughout the year! Your Grace People can serve not only as a fun project to do together as a family, but as a visual reminder of your learning and growth in your love for Jesus.

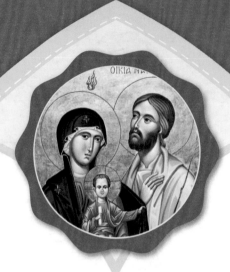

YOUR
Catholic Home
PRAYER BEFORE MEALS

Praying before meals is a loving, simple, and practical way to interweave your faith into your home each day.

Practice it!

If your family is not already in the habit of asking God's blessing before you begin a meal, start saying this prayer before meals together at breakfast, lunch, and dinner. Begin with the Sign of the Cross, and then say:

> Bless us O Lord, and these thy gifts, Which we are about to receive, from thy bounty, Through Christ, Our Lord. Amen.

Make your mealtimes even more serene by ensuring that no one begins eating until the prayer is said, and that the prayer is said only when everyone is seated and quiet. As your children learn the prayer by heart, take turns leading the prayer. Typically the leader begins by saying, "Bless us, O Lord," and then the rest of the prayer is said all together.

ACTIVITY 1

Bible Basics
SCRIPTURE WORKSHEET

Age Level: All ages
Recommended time: 10 minutes
What you need: Bible Basics (**page 4** in the children's activity book)

What you need to know before you begin:

The Old Testament begins with the book of Genesis. You may have heard its opening words, "In the beginning." The Old Testament tells the story of how God created the world, Adam and Eve's fall from grace, and how God entered into covenants with His Chosen People, the Israelites. Broadly speaking, the Old Testament includes the Pentateuch (the first five books of the Old Testament called the Torah by the Jews), the historical books, the wisdom books, and the books of the prophets.

The New Testament tells the story of our Savior, Jesus Christ, and the New Covenant in His Blood. God loved the world so much that He sent His Son, Jesus Christ, to die for our sins and open Heaven to us. The New Testament was written by the Apostles or their immediate disciples. It begins with the four Gospels—Matthew, Mark, Luke, and John—which tell the story of Christ's life from the Annunciation to the Resurrection. Following the Gospels is the book of the Acts of the Apostles, which tells the story of how the Apostles set up the early Church. Following this are 21 epistles, or letters to particular churches in the ancient world. The final book is Revelation, a prophecy about the Apocalypse (end times).

NOTE Catholic Bibles have seven more Old Testament books than Protestant bibles because during the Reformation, Protestants removed seven books that had been part of the Bible since the beginning of Church history.

Activity

Spend time familiarizing yourself and your children with your Bible. Go over the information above with your children and have them complete **Bible Basics (page 4 in the children's activity book)**.

Fill-in-the-Blank Answers:

1. Old, New
2. Genesis, "In the beginning"
3. Five
4. Jesus
5. Apostles

6. Matthew, Mark, Luke, John
7. Acts
8. Epistles
9. Revelation

OT/NT Answers:

1. OT	5. NT	9. OT	13. NT	17. NT
2. NT	6. OT	10. NT	14. NT	18. OT
3. NT	7. OT	11. OT	15. NT	19. OT
4. OT	8. NT	12. NT	16. OT	20. NT

ACTIVITY 2

Basic Catholic Prayers
FAMILY PRAYER ACTIVITY

Age Level: All ages

Recommended time: 10 minutes

What you need: Basic Catholic Prayers (**page 6** in the children's activity book)

Activity

Have your children turn to **Basic Catholic Prayers (page 6 in the children's activity book).** Together with your children, pray the Our Father, the Hail Mary, and the Glory Be, then work on committing them to memory.

Our Father

Our Father, Who art in Heaven, hallowed be Thy name; Thy Kingdom come, Thy will be done on earth as it is in Heaven. Give us this day our daily bread; and forgive us our trespasses as we forgive those who trespass against us; and lead us not into temptation, but deliver us from evil. AMEN.

Hail Mary

Hail Mary, full of grace. The Lord is with thee. Blessed art thou among women, and blessed is the fruit of thy womb, Jesus. Holy Mary, Mother of God, pray for us sinners, now and at the hour of our death. AMEN.

Glory Be

Glory be to the Father, and to the Son, and to the Holy Spirit. As it was in the beginning, is now, and ever shall be, world without end. AMEN.

October
OVERVIEW

VERSE OF THE MONTH

1 JOHN 4:8

Whoever is without love does not know God, for God is love.

SAINT OF THE MONTH

ST. THÉRÈSE OF LISIEUX

LESSON 1

GOD IS THE SOURCE OF ALL LIFE

Overview

The aim of this lesson is for your children to understand that God is the Creator of everything that is, including everything we can see and everything we cannot see. God is the source of all life, and everything good comes from Him. Your children will also begin to understand that God communicates invisible, spiritual realities to us through visible, material signs and symbols in creation.

Catechism Articles to Read

› 1086–1089

› 1114

› 1116

Words to Know

› Creator

› Visible

› Invisible

› Sign

› Symbol

LESSON 2

WHAT IS A SACRAMENT?

Overview

God is the source of all life, and in the Sacraments of the Church, we receive the free and undeserved gift of God's very life – grace. The Church is a visible sign of God's love and of the communion between God and humanity. The seven Sacraments are signs instituted by Christ to give grace.

Catechism Articles to Read

› 1066-1134

› 1210

Words to Know

› Sacrament

› Grace

BY THE END OF THIS MONTH, YOUR CHILDREN SHOULD BE ABLE TO:

✓ Recite this month's Scripture Memorization

✓ Define this month's Words to Know

✓ Explain that God created everything out of nothing and that He is the source of all life

✓ Understand that God helps us understand invisible, spiritual things through visible, material things

✓ Describe, in basic terms, what a Sacrament is

✓ Tell you about St. Thérèse of Lisieux

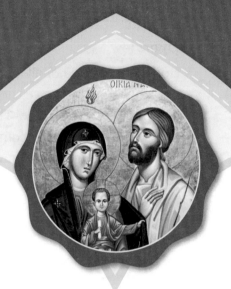

YOUR
Catholic Home
FAMILY PRAYER CORNER

Jesus is the heart of a Catholic home, and a very important and special part of your relationship with Him is prayer. Prayer is a conversation with God that St. Thérèse of Lisieux described as "a surge of the heart." Having a special place where parents and children gather to pray will go a long way toward helping you make prayer a regular part of your family life.

Practice It!

If you do not already have a dedicated place set aside for your family to pray, create a simple prayer space this month. Set up a "prayer corner" in your kitchen or family room on a mantle, a small table, or simply a special shelf in a bookcase. Add a crucifix, a candle, and an icon or two. Two icons that you can cut out and frame are provided in this book on **page 39**.

Celebrate!

ST. THÉRÈSE OF LISIEUX
OCTOBER 1

I am little, but I can aim at being a saint.
–St. Thérèse of Lisieux

THINGS TO DO THIS MONTH:

1 Keep a "Little Ways" journal. Write down all the little ways you show love to God and neighbor each day.

2 Spend time at your parish church and look for all the ways God uses visible things to communicate about invisible things.

VERSE OF THE MONTH
1 JOHN 4:8

Whoever is without love does not know God, for God is love.

REMEMBER!
A Sacrament is a sign instituted by Christ to give grace.

MEMORIZE! The seven Sacraments of the Church are Baptism, Confirmation, Holy Eucharist, Penance and Reconciliation, Anointing of the Sick, Holy Orders, and Holy Matrimony.

ST. THÉRÈSE OF LISIEUX

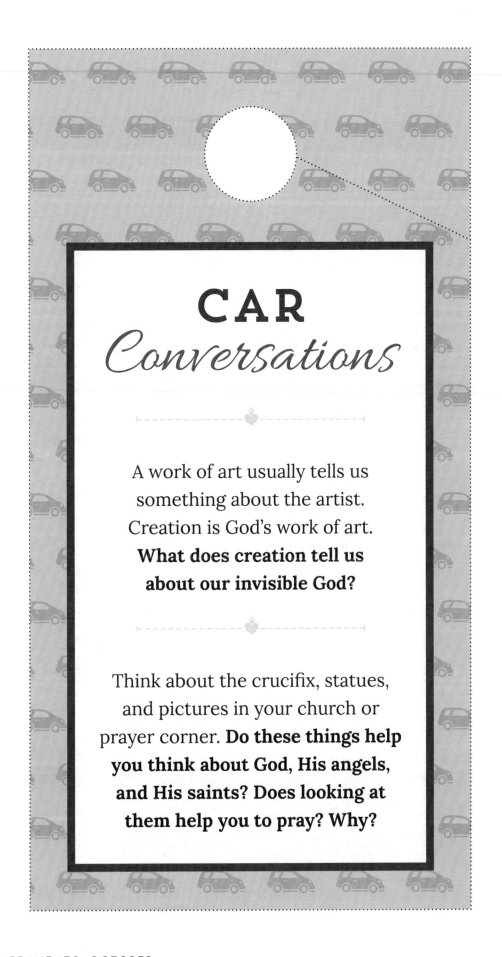

CAR
Conversations

A work of art usually tells us something about the artist. Creation is God's work of art. **What does creation tell us about our invisible God?**

Think about the crucifix, statues, and pictures in your church or prayer corner. **Do these things help you think about God, His angels, and His saints? Does looking at them help you to pray? Why?**

LESSON 1

GOD IS THE SOURCE OF ALL LIFE

Activities and Key Concepts

Activities you will do with your children	Key concepts the activity will teach	Recommended age and time
God Made All Things, Visible and Invisible Family discussion	Invisible things exist.	**Ages:** All ages **Time:** 5 minutes
Ordinary Signs Discussion and activity	A sign points to the existence of something else.	**Ages:** Ages 8 and up **Time:** 10–15 minutes

WORDS TO KNOW

The Words to Know are words that you and your children should know and understand at the end of this month. Use your best judgment about which words to expect each of your children to learn. For older children, you may want to have them create flashcards to help them remember what they have learned.

Creator	Someone who makes something that did not exist before.
Visible	Able to be seen.
Invisible	Unable to be seen.
Sign	A thing that points to the existence of something else. For example, smoke is a sign of fire; a fever is a sign of illness.
Symbol	A thing that represents or stands for something else. For example, a dove is a symbol of the Holy Spirit.

Please choose from the activities for the month.

It is not necessary to complete every activity. We offer a wealth of activities to choose from because each child learns differently, so select the activities that best suit the learning needs of you family. Feel free to shorten or improvise on each activity as necessary. You know best what your family needs!

ACTIVITY 1

God Made All Things, Visible and Invisible
FAMILY DISCUSSION

Age Level: All ages
Recommended time: 5 minutes

What you need to know before you begin:

God is the Creator of all things, both visible and invisible, which He created out of nothing. The book of Genesis opens with some of the most famous words in the Bible, "In the beginning, when God created the heavens and the earth…" The sacred author goes on to describe how God made all things, the material and the spiritual, out of nothing, with only the power of His voice. Given this doctrine, we can understand the sacred author as saying that in the beginning, when God created all that is, visible and invisible, there was nothing but God Himself, who spoke creation into existence. All of creation, therefore, owes its existence to God. God created everything so that the invisible might be made visible.

God creating the Sun, the Moon and the Stars, by Jan Brueghel the Younger.

Discussion

A. Explain to your children that God created everything that exists out of nothing. Then ask them, "What are some of the visible things God created?" Ask older children to write their answers on a separate sheet of paper before you continue. For example, visible creation includes oceans, mountains, rocks, plants, animals, our bodies, and so forth.

B. Next, explain that God created both things you can see and things that you can't see. Ask your children, "What are some of the invisible things He has created?" Older children should again write their answers. Examples of invisible creation includes air, wind, angels, love, our minds, our souls, and so forth.

C. Have your children share their answers, then have a family discussion about how the world that God created includes both visible and invisible things. Within each of us are visible and invisible things. We can see our bodies; we cannot see our souls. But they are real. Ironically, younger children may have an easier time with this teaching! Older children may have a tougher time with it, because they may need to "unlearn" the common notion that things must be seen to be believed.

NOTE   Your children may ask, "Did God create evil?" The simple answer to this question is no. Everything that God creates is good; therefore, He did not create evil.

Ultimately, evil is not a thing. Evil is the absence of good, as darkness is the absence of light. Therefore, evil comes about when we choose anything other than the good. God did not and does not create evil. We do when we fail to choose the good.

 Connection to the Catechism

The sacraments are efficacious signs of grace, instituted by Christ and entrusted to the Church, by which divine life is dispensed to us. (CCC 1131)

BONUS ACTIVITY
Things We Know Are Real but We Cannot See

Age Level: Older children
Recommended time: 5-8 minutes
What you will need: Things We Know Are Real but We Cannot See (**page 9** in the children's activity book)

Ask your children what are some things that they know are real, even though they cannot be seen. Then talk with them about the ways we can know these invisible things are real.

For example, we cannot see the wind, yet we know it is real. How? We can hear it sometimes. We can see the movement of trees as the wind moves through them. We can see things blow around on the ground as the wind blows. Sometimes when the wind is really strong, as in a storm, we can see the damage to buildings that it leaves behind. Another example is love. Love is invisible, but we know it is real because we feel it in our hearts. We express it through hugs, words, and daily sacrifices for each other.

Have your older children turn to **Things We Know Are Real but We Cannot See (page 9 in the children's activity book)** and write three things they know are real even though they can't be seen. Then, for each thing they list, have them think of the ways they know those invisible things are real. Other possible responses include hot and cold, feelings, thoughts, gravity, your breath, and so on. (God is also a possible answer.)

Ordinary Signs
DISCUSSION AND ACTIVITY

Age Level: Ages 8 and up

Recommended time: 10-15 minutes

What you need: Signs of What? (**page 10** in the children's activity book), Signs Charades Cards (**page 35** in this guide)

Discussion

A. Talk with your children about how, as human beings we use signs or symbols constantly. Talk to your children about signs that they use or know about in their daily lives, and what they tell us. Some examples might be:

  › The number of candles on a birthday cake tells us how many years a person has lived.

  › The colored leaves on the trees tell us that summer is ending and fall has arrived.

  › A hug from someone tells you that they love you.

  › Raising your hand in class when the teacher asks a question tells her that you want to answer the question.

B. Now ask your children to turn to **Signs of What? (page 10 in the children's activity book)**. For each picture of a sign, have them write a sentence explaining what each sign tells us. Suggested answers are:

  › Picture of smoke: sign of a fire

  › Picture of a high thermometer: sign of a fever or that someone is sick

  › Picture of birds flying south: sign that winter is coming

  › Picture of two people hugging: sign that they love one another

C. Finish your discussion by pointing out that a sign is a thing that points to the existence of something else. Signs let us know something else exists even if we can't see it.

Game

In order to reinforce the idea that we use signs and symbols in every day life, play a game of Signs Charades. Cut out the eight cards on **Signs Charades Cards (page 35 in this guide)** then shuffle the cards and place them facedown. The first player draws a card and acts out the symbol listed on the card. (For example, one might express the symbol for approval by clapping.) The first person who identifies the symbol receives one point. Continue to take turns performing the charades until all the cards are used up. The person who finishes with the most points is the winner.

LESSON 2

WHAT IS A SACRAMENT?

Activities and Key Concepts

Activities you will do with your children	Key concepts the activity will teach	Recommended age and time
What Is a Sacrament? Discussion and reading	A Sacrament is a visible sign instituted by Christ to give grace.	**Ages:** All ages **Time:** 10–12 minutes
The Sacraments Are Extraordinary Signs Discussion and activity	The Sacraments are signs that actually bring about what they represent.	**Ages:** All ages **Time:** 10 minutes
The Sacraments Are Vehicles of God's Grace Discussion and creative activity	Grace is the gift of God's life in us. We need God's grace to go to Heaven.	**Ages:** All ages **Time:** 10–15 minutes
The Seven Sacraments Discussion and activity	The seven Sacraments were given to the Church by Christ.	**Ages:** All ages **Time:** 5 minutes
Grace Person Introductory activity	Review of the definition of Sacrament.	**Ages:** All ages **Time:** 5 minutes

LESSON 2

WORDS TO KNOW

The Words to Know are words that you and your children should know and understand at the end of this month. Use your best judgment about which words to expect each of your children to learn. For older children, you may want to have them create flashcards to help them remember what they have learned.

Sacrament	A visible sign instituted by Christ to give grace. There are seven Sacraments: Baptism, Confirmation, Eucharist, Penance and Reconciliation, Anointing of the Sick, Marriage, and Holy Orders.
Grace	The gift of God's life in us.

What Is a Sacrament?
DISCUSSION AND READING

Age Level: All ages, with a reading for children 8 and up

Recommended time: 10-12 minutes

What you need: What Is a Sacrament? (**page 11** in the children's activity book)

What you need to know before you begin:

Throughout Salvation History, no one had ever seen God, but God made Himself known by giving His people visible signs. Visible signs like a marriage between a man and woman (the sign of His promise to Adam and Eve), the rainbow (the sign of His promise to Noah), and the Law (in the tablets of the Ten Commandments), all took on greater meaning in their communication of God's love and mercy.

Then finally, at the appointed time, God made Himself visible – He entered into human history by sending His only, beloved Son, the Second Person of the Blessed Trinity, to become human, like us in all things but sin. Jesus fully revealed the Father – the people of Jesus' time could then see God, touch God, hear God, be healed by God, be fed by God, and be embraced by God. And, when the time came, Jesus poured out His love for us by sacrificing Himself on the Cross, paying the debt of sin that we could not and pouring out grace.

And even though Jesus could not remain with us here on earth, He promised us in Matthew 28:20: "I am with you always, until the end of the age." But if Jesus ascended into Heaven and sits at the right hand of the Father, how can He still be with us here on earth? The answer is that Jesus continues to be with us, in and through the Church, as she dispenses through the Sacraments the graces He won on the Cross. As we celebrate and receive the Sacraments, we receive the grace poured out from His sacrifice and are able to experience the fullness of God in our lives.

In this age of the Church, which Jesus Himself founded during His earthly life to carry on His mission of salvation of all souls, we continue in the tradition of our spiritual ancestors by recognizing certain signs and symbols as having the power to communicate God's love to us. The Seven Sacraments of the Church – Baptism, Confirmation, Holy Eucharist, Penance and Reconciliation, Anointing of the Sick, Holy Orders, and Holy Matrimony – all instituted by Christ, are efficacious signs of God's grace. This means that each Sacrament not only is a visible representation of God's love and life, but also effects, or causes, God's grace to be present. The Sacraments, in fact, are the primary means for us to receive grace, particularly by frequent reception of the Eucharist.

Discussion

A. Recall with your children the discussion you had about signs, and point out how God Himself uses signs and symbols, too! Specifically, He gives us grace through physical signs and symbols. We call these the Sacraments.

B. Using the information that you read before beginning this activity, explain to your children what a Sacrament is. Make sure to include these three important things about the Sacraments:

1. They are efficacious signs of God's grace. This means that each Sacrament not only is a visible representation of God's love and life, but also effects, or causes, God's grace to be present.

2. They are given to us by Jesus.

3. They are the primary means for us to receive grace.

C. For older children, have them read **What Is a Sacrament? (page 11 in the children's activity book)**. Then discuss with them what they read.

The Sacraments Are Extradorinary Signs
DISCUSSION AND ACTIVITY

Age Level: All ages

Recommended time: 10 minutes

What you need: The Sacraments Are Extraordinary Signs (**page 12** in the children's activity book)

What you need to know before you begin:

You have learned all about signs and symbols in everyday life, or ordinary signs. But the Sacraments are not ordinary signs – they are different from every other sign in the world. This is because the Sacraments are signs that can actually bring about what they represent. Ordinary signs can't do this. For example, smoke can tell us that fire exists, but it does not cause fire. Or birds flying south can be a sign of winter coming, but they do not cause winter to come.

Activity

A. Have your children turn to **The Sacraments Are Extraordinary Signs (page 12 in the children's activity book)**.

B. Talk with your children about what you read and go over the examples on the children's activity page of how the Sacraments actually bring about what they represent:

> **Baptism** is a sign of cleansing from sin, and it causes cleansing from sin.

> **Confirmation** is a sign of strengthening, and it causes our souls to be strengthened.

> **The Eucharis**t is a sign of Jesus' sacrifice on the Cross, and it actually makes His sacrifice present for us again. It is sign of unity among Christians, and it causes that unity to come about.

The Seven Sacraments (detail), by Rogier van der Weyden.

> **Confession** is a sign of God's forgiveness, and it actually causes that forgiveness.

> **Anointing of the Sick** is a sign of God's healing mercy, and it actually brings about that healing.

> **Holy Orders** is a sign of Christ's ministry on earth, and it actually brings His ministry to us through called men who receive this Sacrament.

> **Holy Matrimony** is a sign of a man's and a woman's lifelong commitment, and it actually causes their union to become permanent.

C. Finally, have your children complete the worksheet, reviewing the pictures of signs and crossing out any ordinary signs.

Answers: The birthday party, graduation, and picnic are crossed out. The Baptism, anointing, and marriage are all Sacraments, so they should NOT be crossed out.

 Connection to the Catechism

...The seven sacraments touch all the stages and all the important moments of Christian life: they give birth and increase, healing and mission to the Christian's life of faith. There is thus a certain resemblance between the stages of natural life and the stages of the spiritual life. (CCC 1210)

ACTIVITY 3

The Sacraments Are Vehicles of God's Grace

DISCUSSION AND CREATIVE ACTIVITY

Age Level: All ages

Recommended time: 10-15 minutes

What you need: Jesus' Gift of Grace in the Sacraments (**page 14** in the children's activity book)

What you need to know before you begin:

Grace is the gift of God's life in us. Grace is necessary for us to persevere on the path of holiness, to avoid sin, and ultimately to attain Heaven. In His divine wisdom, Jesus gave us the gift of the seven Sacraments as visible, material means of receiving the invisible grace of God.

There are several types of grace:

› We receive **sanctifying grace** to make us holy and help us get to Heaven.

› **Sacramental graces** are the graces we receive that are specific to each Sacrament.

› We receive **actual grace** to help us in particular situations to do good and avoid evil. (This is easy to remember because the word actual contains the word act. Actual grace helps us to act rightly.)

Discussion

A. Have your children think about the best gift they ever received, and think of reasons why it was the best one.

B. Explain that God gives us gifts too and that the gifts God gives us are greater than any other gift we could receive! Grace is the gift of God's life in us. It is help that

God gives us to respond to His call to holiness. The only reason He gives us this gift is because He loves us. We do nothing to deserve or "earn" it.

C. Go over the definition of grace: the gift of God's life in us. It is the undeserved help that God gives us to respond to His call to holiness. We need grace to help us become holy, to avoid sin, and attain Heaven. And Jesus gave us the gift of the Sacraments as a way of receiving God's grace.

D. Finally, go over the types of graces that you read about:

> Sanctifying grace

> Sacramental graces

> Actual grace

Activity

Have your children turn to **Jesus' Gift of Grace in the Sacraments (page 14 in the children's activity book).** As your children color the pictures, read the information aloud to them. Talk with them about how each of the Sacraments is a sign of God's grace that actually makes His grace present to us. The Sacraments work this way because Jesus is present in them. In other words, in Baptism, it is Jesus who baptizes. In Anointing of the Sick, it is Jesus who anoints. Jesus works through the priest or minister in order to make the effects of the Sacraments present. Although we hear the priest speaking words of absolution in Confession, it is Jesus who forgives us.

 Connection to the Catechism

The visible rites by which the sacraments are celebrated signify and make present the graces proper to each sacrament. They bear fruit in those who receive them with the required dispositions. (CCC 1131)

ACTIVITY 4

The Seven Sacraments
DISCUSSION AND ACTIVITY

Age Level: All ages

Recommended time: 5 minutes

What you need: Signs of the Sacraments (**page 18** in the children's activity book), markers and/or crayons

Discussion

Explain to your children that the Sacraments were given to the Church by Christ. It is in and through the Church that the Sacraments are given to us. The Church celebrates seven Sacraments:

Sacraments of Initiation	**Sacraments of Healing**	**Sacraments at the Service of Communion**
Baptism	Penance and	
Confirmation	Reconciliation	Marriage
Eucharist	Anointing of the Sick	Holy Orders

Activity

Have your children turn to **Signs of the Sacraments (page 18 in the children's activity book)**. Work together with your children to fill in the chart. As you are completing the chart, be sure to remind your children that the Sacraments are extraordinary signs – they don't just point to something else, they actually effect change in our life and in our souls.

Answers:

1. Water

2. God

3. Body and Blood

4. Forgiveness

5. Sick

6. Holy Orders

7. Lifelong (or permanent, indissoluble)

BONUS ACTIVITY
Sacraments Word Search

Age Level: Ages 8 and up

Recommended time: 5-10 minutes

What you will need: Sacraments Word Search (**page 19** in the children's activity book)

Have your older children complete a fun word search. As they work, talk to them about what the words mean, and/or ask your children to recall the definitions of the words.

 ## Connection to the Catechism

The Church celebrates the sacraments as a priestly community structured by the baptismal priesthood and the priesthood of ordained ministers. (CCC 1132)

ACTIVITY 5

Grace Person
INTRODUCTORY ACTIVITY

Age Level: All ages

Recommended time: 5 minutes

What you need: Grace Person Template (**page 20** in the children's activity book), posterboard or foam core, markers and/or crayons

This month you will trace and cut out the figure of a human being: your "Grace Person." You may choose to do one figure for your whole family, or you may create a grace person to represent each person in your family. Throughout this year, you will create decorations and adornments representing the Sacraments to put on your Grace Person. At the end of the year you will have a representation of the way all seven Sacraments give us grace at important times in our lives.

Activity

This month, create your Grace Person. Get a large piece of poster board or foam core from an office-supply or hobby store. Have your children tear out the **Grace Person Template (page 20 in the children's activity book)**, cut it out, trace the template onto posterboard or foam core, and cut if out. Then have your children draw basic features: hair, a face, basic clothing, and shoes. Keep these very simple, as you will be adding symbols and text to your Grace Person throughout the year.

Once you have each completed your Grace Person, write the definition of a Sacrament on the back: "A Sacrament is a visible sign instituted by Christ to give grace."

St. Thérèse of Lisieux
SAINT OF THE MONTH

Age level: All ages

Recommended time: 5 minutes

What you need: St. Thérèse of Lisieux (**page 21** in the children's activity book), markers and/or crayons

Activity

Read aloud the story of this month's saint to your children. You may also want to show them the full page saint image. While you are reading or sometime the next day, have them complete the coloring page on **page 22** of the children's activity book.

Biography of St. Thérèse of Lisieux

THÉRÈSE MARTIN was born in Alençon, France. Her mother and father had nine children, and Thérèse was one of five who survived. Thérèse's mother died when Thérèse was only four years old. Her father moved the family to Lisieux, and Thérèse's older sisters helped take care of her.

For much of her life, Thérèse was delicate and sensitive. She would cry if she thought someone was criticizing her. Then she would feel even worse about herself because she had cried.

Two of her sisters were nuns in a Discalced Carmelite convent. Thérèse also received a call to religious life, but she was too young to join the convent. But she did not give up. When she was 15, she went on a pilgrimage to Rome. Her group was able to visit the pope, and she asked him for special permission to enter the convent. One of the pope's officers saw her and was impressed with her courage. She was given permission to enter the convent. Thérèse would be a cloistered nun, meaning she would spend her days in prayer, away from other people and the world.

Thérèse knew that Jesus wanted the little ones to come to Him. In fact, Jesus Himself had become a child! So Thérèse was glad she was little. Thérèse also wanted to be holy. At first she felt discouraged when she compared herself with the saints. But instead of staying discouraged, she persevered. She wrote: "In spite of my littleness, I can aim at being a saint. ... I will look for some means of going to heaven by a little way which is very short and very straight, a little way that is quite new." St. Thérèse is known for this "Little Way" of seeking holiness in ordinary, everyday things.

Thérèse loved the Sacraments and recalled her first Holy Communion. She said, "How sweet was that first kiss of Jesus! It was a kiss of love; I felt that I was loved, and I said: 'I love You, and I give myself to you forever!'" Thérèse would often spend time in adoration of the Blessed Sacrament. The Blessed Sacrament is another name for the Eucharist — the Body and Blood of Christ.

In 1896 Thérèse developed tuberculosis, which is a painful and deadly illness. She died less than a year later at age 24. The wisdom in her writings was so profound that Pope John Paul II named her a Doctor of the Church.

SIGNS CHARADES CARDS

Cut out the cards to use in the Signs Charades game.

Stop	Peace
Strength	Nervousness
Christian	Joy

Friendship

Approval

Happiness

Sadness

Fear

Love

PRAYER CORNER ICONS

Tear out the next two pages, then cut out the icons and insert into a
5"x7" frame to begin to build your own family prayer corner.

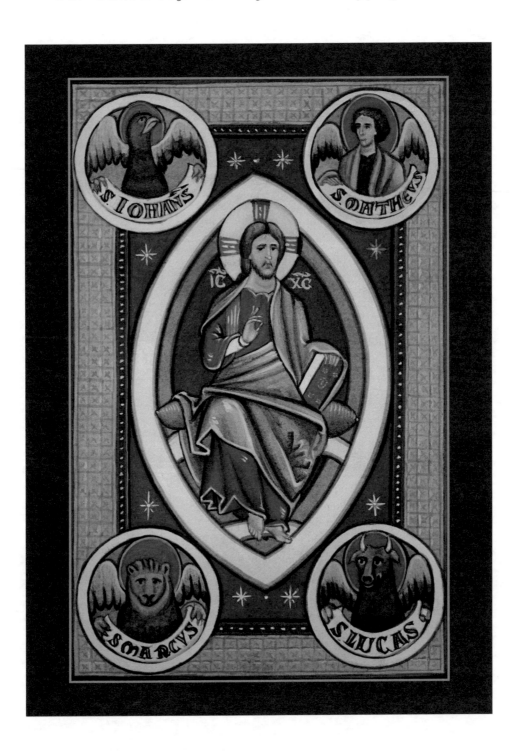

October in Review

THIS MONTH YOU EXPLORED AS A FAMILY THE QUESTIONS:

Where does all life come from?

How does God help us understand invisible things?

What is a Sacrament?

In Lesson 1 your children learned:

> Sacraments are signs that bring about what they represent.

> The seven Sacraments are visible signs, instituted by Christ and entrusted to the Church, to give grace.

> We need grace, the free gift of God's life in us, to go to Heaven.

In Lesson 2 your children learned:

> God is the creator of all things visible and invisible.

> A sign is something that points to the existence of something else.

In this space below, write some reflections about the past month. What was your favorite activity? What didn't go as well? Will you adjust anything about what you're doing? What special intentions do you have for next month?

November
OVERVIEW

VERSE OF THE MONTH

JOHN 3:5

Jesus answered, "Amen, amen I say to you, no one can enter the Kingdom of God without being born of water and Spirit."

SAINT OF THE MONTH

ST. CATHERINE OF ALEXANDRIA

LESSON 3

THE SACRAMENTS OF INITIATION

Overview

The aim of this lesson is for your children to understand what it means to be initiated into something, as well as how and why the Sacraments of Initiation bring them into the fullness of the Christian life.

Catechism Articles to Read

- ➤ 849
- ➤ 1115-1116
- ➤ 1120
- ➤ 1128
- ➤ 1131
- ➤ 1212
- ➤ 1535
- ➤ 2013

Words to Know

- ➤ To Initiate
- ➤ Vocation
- ➤ Evangelize
- ➤ Gospel

LESSON 4

BAPTISM

Overview

In this lesson your children explore the gateway to the Christian life: Baptism. In Baptism, your children were cleansed of the stain of Original Sin and became part of God's family.

Catechism Articles to Read

> 1213-1284

Words to Know

> Baptism
> Form
> Matter
> Recipient
> Effect

BY THE END OF THIS MONTH, YOUR CHILDREN SHOULD BE ABLE TO:

✔ Recite this month's Scripture Memorization

✔ Define this month's Words to Know

✔ Explain what it means to be "initiated"

✔ Understand what Baptism is and how it affects us

✔ Tell you about St. Catherine of Alexandria

YOUR
Catholic Home
HOLY WATER

Have you ever noticed where the baptismal font is usually located in a cathedral? You will find it near the entrance. This placement signifies that we enter the Christian life through Baptism. We also find fonts of Holy Water near the doors of church buildings. When we enter a church, we dip our fingers in the Holy Water and make the Sign of the Cross. This ritual is meant to help us recall our Baptism and our need for Christ's cleansing.

Practice It!

Bring Holy Water and all of its spiritual benefits into your family life by placing a Holy Water font near the entrance to your home. (To fill it, you can ask your priest to bless water for you, or ask permission to fill a small bottle from your parish baptismal font.) Use the water in the home font to bless yourselves as you come and go each day, to bless the rooms of your house, your children's school things, even your car!

Celebrate!

ST. CATHERINE OF ALEXANDRIA
NOVEMBER 25

I have become a bride of Christ.
—*St. Catherine of Alexandria*

THINGS TO DO THIS MONTH:

1 Mark your calendars with the dates of your family members' Baptisms. Celebrate these days even more than you would a birthday!

2 Bring the blessings of holy water into your home with a small font near your front door.

VERSE OF THE MONTH
JOHN 3:5

Jesus answered, "Amen, amen, I say to you, no one can enter the Kingdom of God without being born of water and Spirit."

REMEMBER!
Because of the Sacraments of Initiation, we are given the same vocation as all of Christ's disciples: holiness and evangelization. The word *evangelize* means to share the Good News of Jesus Christ with others.

MEMORIZE!
Through Baptism we are freed from sin and reborn as sons of God; we become members of Christ and are incorporated into the Church and made sharers in her mission.

ST. CATHERINE OF ALEXANDRIA

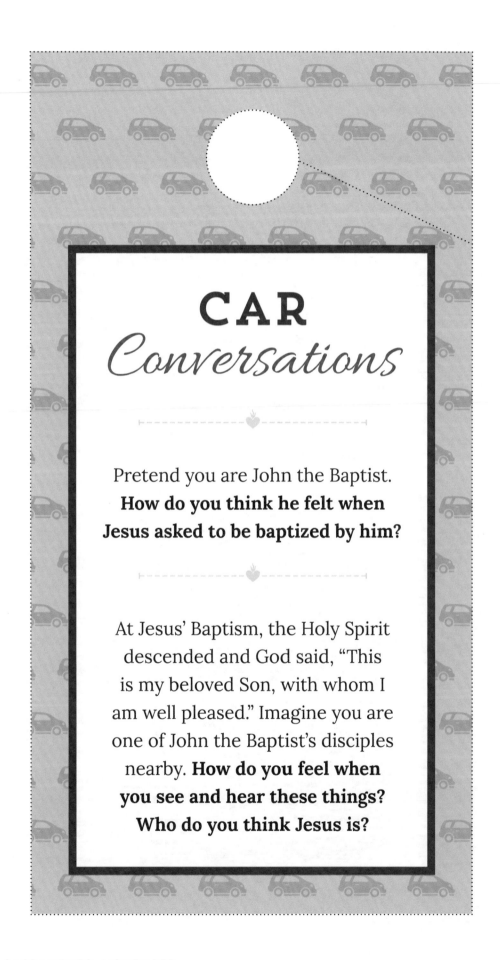

CAR
Conversations

Pretend you are John the Baptist. **How do you think he felt when Jesus asked to be baptized by him?**

At Jesus' Baptism, the Holy Spirit descended and God said, "This is my beloved Son, with whom I am well pleased." Imagine you are one of John the Baptist's disciples nearby. **How do you feel when you see and hear these things? Who do you think Jesus is?**

LESSON 3

THE SACRAMENTS OF INITIATION

Activities and Key Concepts

Activities you will do with your children	Key concepts the activity will teach	Recommended age and time
What Is an Initiation? Family discussion	The Sacraments of Initiation make us members of the Church, strengthen us for our life's journey, and give us our vocation as Christians.	**Ages:** All ages **Time:** 10 minutes
The Vocation of a Christian Reading and discussion	We are all called to be holy and to share the Gospel.	**Ages:** All ages **Time:** 10 minutes

LESSON 3

WORDS TO KNOW

The Words to Know are words that you and your children should know and understand at the end of this month. Use your best judgment about which words to expect each of your children to learn. For older children, you may want to have them create flashcards to help them remember what they have learned.

To Initiate	To formally make a person part of a group.
Vocation	The calling of God in which we love and serve Him.
Evangelize	To share the Gospel, or the Good News of Jesus Christ, with others.
Gospel	The Good News of Jesus Christ.

Please choose from the activities for the month.

It is not necessary to complete every activity. We offer a wealth of activities to choose from because each child learns differently, so select the activities that best suit the learning needs of you family. Feel free to shorten or improvise on each activity as necessary. You know best what your family needs!

ACTIVITY 1

What Is an Initiation?
FAMILY DISCUSSION

Age Level: All ages
Recommended time: 10 minutes

What you need to know before you begin:

The Church has seven Sacraments. Of those seven Sacraments, we recognize three as the Sacraments of Initiation because they introduce us to and make us members of the Church, strengthen us for our life's journey, and give us our vocation, or calling, as Christians.

To be initiated means formally to become a part of a group or society. In general, initiations may involve taking an oath, passing a challenge, or enduring a trial. Then upon initiation, the person has a common bond with other members and is given a role or mission. The Sacraments of Initiation resemble this pattern. The Christian life begins with baptismal promises, and then through God's grace we are made members of Christ's Body, the Church. We receive the mission shared by all disciples of Christ to become holy, and to bring the Good News to the world. In Confirmation our baptismal grace is perfected, and we receive a strengthening of the gifts of the Holy Spirit. In the Eucharist, the source and summit of the Christian life, we receive the very Body and Blood of Our Lord Jesus Christ, which nourishes us in our mission to evangelize. We will learn more about these Sacraments throughout the year.

Discussion

A. Ask your children to recall a time when they were made part of a group. They may also think of examples from family members' lives. For example:

> - their first day of kindergarten
> - their first Cub Scout or American Heritage Girls meeting
> - the day they became part of a sports team
> - older siblings or cousins who matriculated at universities
> - older siblings or cousins who married
> - older siblings or cousins who joined the military

B. Now ask your child what promise(s) or challenge(s) accompanied this transition, and what new roles or missions came with it. (Not every example will follow this exact pattern, but the point is to look for patterns/similarities.) For example:

> - Once in kindergarten, she has to obey the class rules (promise) and is now a student (new role) with the job of learning (mission).
> - At the first Cub Scout meeting, he would have had to take an oath to do his best (promise) and is now a Cub Scout (new role) with the mission of preparing to make morally upright choices (mission).
> - A single woman promises to be true to one man (promise) and is now a wife (new role) with the purpose of helping her husband get to Heaven and welcoming children into their family (mission).
> - A young man takes the enlistment oath and completes training (promise and challenge) and is now a Marine (new role) with the responsibility of defending our nation (mission).

C. Connect this pattern with the Sacraments of Initiation: Baptism, Confirmation, and the Eucharist. Ask your children to recall the definition of a Sacrament: a visible sign instituted by Christ to give grace. The Sacraments of Initiation are called that because they introduce us to and make us members of the Church, strengthen us for our life's journey, and give us our vocation, or mission, as Christians.

> **NOTE** ▶ You may wish to discuss with your older children how the desire for initiation ceremonies/rites of passage transcends human cultures. They have been part of every human society throughout history. When God is a part of these rituals, such as in Baptism, or Holy Matrimony, they are always full of love. When God is left out of them, we see bad practices such as hazing, violent gang initiations, binge drinking, and so forth. These are sinful actions we must avoid. No group that is worth being a part of would expect or demand a violent and hurtful initiation.

BONUS ACTIVITY
Initiation Creative Activity

Age Level: Younger children
Recommended time: 10-15 minutes
What you will need: Initiation (**page 26** in the children's activity book)

Have your children draw a picture depicting a time they were made part of a group (e.g., the first day of kindergarten, Cub Scouts, playing on a team, and so forth). Encourage them to show one or more of the parts of an initiation you identified in your family discussion: a promise made, a new role received, and a new mission begun.

They should then color the page listing the Sacraments of Initiation: Baptism, Confirmation, and Eucharist.

 Connection to the Catechism

The sacraments of Christian initiation – Baptism, Confirmation, and the Eucharist – lay the foundations of every Christian life. ...The faithful are born anew by Baptism, strengthened by the sacrament of Confirmation, and receive in the Eucharist the food of eternal life. By means of these sacraments of Christian initiation, they thus receive in increasing measure the treasures of the divine life and advance toward the perfection of charity. (CCC 1212)

ACTIVITY 2

The Vocation of a Christian
READING AND DISCUSSION

Age Level: All ages

Recommended time: 10 minutes

What you need: The Vocation of a Christian (**page 27** in the children's activity book)

Activity

A. Read the essay on "The Vocation of a Christian" and have a discussion about it with your children. For younger children, go over the main points at a level that they will understand. For older children, you may have them read the essay themselves, then discuss with them what they read. The essay is also in the children's activity book on **page 27.**

B. Make sure to discuss the following points:

- The Sacraments of Initiation give us a vocation (or calling) to holiness and to the mission to bring the Gospel to every person in the world.

- Jesus calls us to be holy – to love Him first above all else and love our neighbors as ourselves. The Sacraments of Initiation strengthen us to be able to become holy.

- Jesus calls us to bring the Good News of His life, Death, and Resurrection to the world.

NOTE The word "evangelize" means to share the Good News of Jesus Christ with others. People often use the word today to mean "pressuring" other people to become Christians. This is not the true meaning! Evangelization is a joyful action. We should use both words and actions to bring the love of Christ to the world.

Sermon on the Mount, by Bl. Fra Angelico.

The Vocation of a Christian Essay

The Sacraments of Initiation are the foundation of the vocation of each Christian person – a vocation to holiness and to the mission of bringing the Gospel to every person in the world. The true home of a Christian is not earth but Heaven.

Our Vocation to Holiness

Jesus tells us in Matthew's Gospel: "So be perfect, just as your heavenly Father is perfect" (5:48). He tells us more about what that means in Matthew 22:37-39: "He said to him, 'You shall love the Lord, your God, with all your heart, with all your soul, and with all your mind. This is the greatest and the first commandment. The second is like it: You shall love your neighbor as yourself.'"

Jesus is telling us that to be perfect as our heavenly Father is perfect means to love Him first above all else and to love our neighbors as ourselves.

We are all called to be holy. Because of the Sacraments of Initiation – Baptism, Confirmation, and the Eucharist – we are given the vocation of holiness that all of Jesus' disciples share, and we are strengthened by the Sacraments of Initiation to be able to attain that holiness. To be perfect as our Heavenly Father is perfect is to be holy. And Jesus then tells how to be holy, which is to obey the two greatest commandments, to love God above all else, and to love our neighbor as ourselves. This is how we become saints.

The Mission to Evangelize

Pope Paul VI wrote that the Church "exists to evangelize." Evangelization is the sharing of the Gospel by word and example of life. Jesus Himself gave the Apostles this mission before He ascended into Heaven. "Then Jesus approached and said to them, 'All power in heaven and on earth has been given to me. Go, therefore, and make disciples of all nations, baptizing them in the name of the Father, and of the Son, and of the Holy Spirit, teaching them to observe all that I have commanded you. And behold, I am with you always, until the end of the age" (Matthew 28:18-20). Evangelization is doing exactly what Jesus commanded His Apostles to do. The Sacraments of Initiation, as we've learned, give us the same vocation as all of Christ's disciples, which includes evangelization.

The word *evangelization* comes from the Latin word *evangelion*, which means "gospel." Our word *gospel* comes from the Greek word *eungelion* which means "good message" or "good news." Although we often use the word *gospel* to mean the four books of the Bible by Matthew, Mark, Luke, and John, the word has a much richer meaning. The gospel is the Good News of Jesus Christ: that He came down from Heaven, died for us on the Cross, and rose from the dead to offer us salvation. At its heart, the call to evangelization means we are called to share the Good News in our lives.

BONUS ACTIVITY
Help Me to Be Holy Prayer

Age Level: All ages
Recommended time: 5 minutes
What you will need: Help Me to Be Holy (**page 30** in the children's activity book)

Have your children write a prayer to the Holy Spirit asking Him to help you grow in holiness as you live out the mission you received at Baptism. For younger children, have him or her dictate the poem to you while you write it down. Then pray it together.

BONUS ACTIVITY
The Mission of a Disciple

Age Level: Older children
Recommended time: 10-15 minutes
What you will need: The Mission of a Disciple (**page 29** in the children's activity book)

Have your older children look up and write out Matthew 5:48 and Matthew 22:37-39. Then help them reflect on the Scripture passages by discussing the following questions:

1. Jesus knows our hearts better than anyone, even better than we know ourselves. He knows that we tend to sin. So how can He ask us to be perfect? *The answer is that He doesn't leave us alone to do it. If we tried to be perfect on our own, we would never succeed. We need Jesus to do it.*

2. To be perfect like our Father in Heaven is to be holy. What does Jesus tell us to do in order to be holy? *"You shall love the Lord, your God, with all your heart, with all your soul, and with all your mind. This is the greatest and the first commandment. The second is like it: You shall love your neighbor as yourself."*

3. What are some ways you can use use both words and actions to bring the love of Christ to the world? *Answers will vary.*

 ## Connection to the Catechism

Baptism, Confirmation, and Eucharist are sacraments of Christian initiation. They ground the common vocation of all Christ's disciples, a vocation to holiness and to the mission of evangelizing the world. They confer the graces needed for the life according to the Spirit during this life as pilgrims on the march towards the homeland. (CCC 1533)

LESSON 4

BAPTISM

Activities and Key Concepts

Activities you will do with your children	Key concepts the activity will teach	Recommended age and time
What Is Baptism? Scripture reading and discussion	Baptism is the gateway to the Christian life	**Ages:** All ages **Time:** 10 minutes
Baptism Prefigured Scripture search	The Great Flood, the parting of the Red Sea, and the crossing of the river Jordan foreshadow Baptism.	**Ages:** Ages 8 and up **Time:** 10 minutes
The Effects of Baptism Activity and Discussion	In Baptism our sins are forgiven, we are reborn in Christ and made sons and daughters of God, made members of the Church, and receive an indelible mark on our souls.	**Ages:** All ages **Time:** 10 minutes
Remembering Your Baptism Discussion and activity	At your Baptism, you were set apart for eternal life with God.	**Ages:** All ages **Time:** 10-15 minutes

LESSON 4

BAPTISM

Activities and Key Concepts
(continued)

Activities you will do with your children	Key concepts the activity will teach	Recommended age and time
Jesus' Baptism Scripture and sacred art activity	Jesus was baptized to teach us the way to salvation.	**Ages:** All ages **Time:** 10 minutes
Baptismal Garment Grace person activity	Review of the meaning of the white baptismal garment.	**Ages:** All ages **Time:** 10 minutes

LESSON 4
WORDS TO KNOW

The Words to Know are words that you and your children should know and understand at the end of this month. Use your best judgment about which words to expect each of your children to learn. For older children, you may want to have them create flashcards to help them remember what they have learned.

Baptism	The first Sacrament, in which we are reborn in Christ through water.
Form	The words spoken in a Sacrament.
Matter	The physical material used in a Sacrament.
Recipient	The person who receives a Sacrament.
Effect	The way a Sacrament changes us.

ACTIVITY 1

What is Baptism?
SCRIPTURE READING AND DISCUSSION

Age Level: All ages
Recommended time: 10 minutes
What you need: Bible

What you need to know before you begin:

The *Catechism of the Catholic Church* provides a simple explanation for what Jesus does for us in Baptism: "Holy Baptism is the basis of the whole Christian life, the gateway to life in the Spirit, and the door which gives access to the other sacraments. Through Baptism we are freed from sin and reborn as sons of God; we become members of Christ, are incorporated into the Church and made sharers in her mission: Baptism is the sacrament of regeneration through water in the word" (CCC 1213).

Baptism is the very participation in the death and resurrection of Jesus Christ. St. Paul told the Church at Rome: "We were therefore buried with him through baptism into death in order that, just as Christ was raised from the dead through the glory of the Father, we too may live a new life" (Romans 6:3-4).

Baptism is necessary for salvation. By our Baptism, we are made new creations – we have "put on Christ" (Galatians 3:27) – and with the support of the whole Christian community, we advance on the journey toward salvation.

Activity

A. Read aloud John 3:1-7 to your children:

Now there was a Pharisee named Nicodemus, a ruler of the Jews. He came to Jesus at night and said to him, "Rabbi, we know that you are a teacher who has come from God, for no one can do these signs that you are doing unless God is with him."

Jesus answered and said to him, "Amen, amen, I say to you, no one can see the kingdom of God without being born from above."

Nicodemus said to him, "How can a person once grown old be born again? Surely he cannot reenter his mother's womb and be born again, can he?"

Jesus answered, "Amen, amen, I say to you, no one can enter the kingdom of God without being born of water and Spirit. What is born of flesh is flesh and what is born of spirit is spirit.Do not be amazed that I told you, 'You must be born from above.'"

B. Then read aloud Mark 16:16:

Whoever believes and is baptized will be saved; whoever does not believe will be condemned.

C. Discuss with your children that Jesus is telling us in Scripture that rebirth in Baptism is necessary to go to Heaven. When we are baptized, we die a spiritual death with Christ and when we come out of the waters, we are reborn in the Spirit. We are reborn as sons and daughters of God, and because of this rebirth, we can now receive the rest of the Sacraments. That is why the *Catechism* calls the Sacrament of Baptism the "gateway to life in the Spirit" and "the door which gives us access to the other Sacraments" (CCC 1213).

 Connection to the Catechism

The fruit of Baptism, or baptismal grace, is a rich reality that includes forgiveness of original sin and all personal sins, birth into the new life by which man becomes an adoptive son of the Father, a member of Christ and a temple of the Holy Spirit. By this very fact the person baptized is incorporated into the Church, the Body of Christ, and made a sharer in the priesthood of Christ. (CCC 279)

BONUS ACTIVITY
Baptism Is the Gateway

Age Level: All ages
Recommended time: 5 minutes
What you will need: Baptism Gateway (**page** 77 of this guide) a piece of light colored construction paper, glue, markers and/or crayons

A. Tear out the Baptism: The Gateway to Life in the Spirit page on **page 77**. CUT along the dotted lines and FOLD along the solid lines (on either side of the large main gate) so that the gate opens outward. Once you fold out the two panels to allow the gates to open, glue the page onto a piece of light colored construction paper. Make sure not to put glue on the gates themselves, or they will not open.

B. Ask your children to recall the names of the other six Sacraments (Confirmation, Eucharist, Penance and Reconciliation, Anointing of the Sick, Marriage, and Holy Orders). Using markers or crayons, have them write the six Sacraments on the construction paper inside the open doors of the gateway.

C. As your children write the names of the Sacraments inside the gateway, explain that in Baptism, we are reborn as sons and daughters of God, and because of this rebirth, we can now receive the rest of the Sacraments. That is why the *Catechism* calls the Sacrament of Baptism the "gateway to life in the Spirit" and "the door which gives us access to the other Sacraments" (CCC 1213).

ACTIVITY 2

Baptism Prefigured
SCRIPTURE SEARCH

Age Level: Ages 8 and up

Recommended time: 10 minutes

What you need: Bible, Baptism Prefigured (**page 31** in the children's activity book)

The Deluge. by Michelangelo.

What you need to know before you begin:

Jesus' Baptism and His commissioning of the Apostles to baptize are the culmination of thousands of years of preparation for the Sacrament, as God prefigured the Sacrament of Initiation throughout His saving work in salvation history.

From the very beginning, when the Spirit of God hovered over the primordial waters, to Noah and the Great Flood, to the crossing of the Red Sea and the River Jordan, we have always understood the signs that have pointed the way to Baptism. God's people pass from chaos, death, slavery, and sin, through powerful and life-giving waters, to new life in grace and freedom as a new creation.

Activity

Ask your older children to turn to **Baptism Prefigured (page 31 in the children's activity book)**. Have them independently look up the Bible verses and write short summaries of the passages, making sure to include who is in the story and what happened. Then, have them connect the stories to Baptism, explaining how God used water in the story just like He uses the waters of Baptism.

Answers:

1. **Genesis 6:5-8, 7:12-21:** The story of Noah and the flood. The world was overrun with wickedness, except for Noah, who was faithful to God. God flooded the earth, wiping out the wicked while saving Noah and his family. God used the waters to "make an end of sin and a new beginning of goodness" (CCC 1219).

2. **Exodus 14: 10-31:** The story of Moses and the Israelites crossing the Red Sea. After leaving Egypt, the Israelites were being pursued by Pharoah and his army. The Israelites cried out to God. He parted the Red Sea, allowing the Israelites to pass on dry ground, then released the waters to flow back on the Egyptians, destroying their army. God used the waters of the Red Sea to free the Israelites just like He uses the waters of Baptism to free us from sin.

3. **Joshua 3:14-17:** The story of the Israelites crossing the Jordan River. When the priests carrying the Ark of the Covenant reached the river and submerged their feet, God held back the water, allowing the Israelites to cross into the Promised Land. God used the water to give the gift of the Promised Land, which is an image of eternal life, to the Israelites just as He gives us the gift of eternal life in Baptism.

 Connection to the Catechism

[T]he Church solemnly commemorates the great events in salvation history that already prefigured the mystery of Baptism....

The Church has seen in Noah's ark a prefiguring of salvation by Baptism, for by it "a few, that is, eight persons, were saved through water"....

[T]he crossing of the Red Sea, literally the liberation of Israel from the slavery of Egypt....

Baptism is prefigured in the crossing of the Jordan River by which the People of God received the gift of the land promised to Abraham's descendants. (CCC 1217-1222)

ACTIVITY 3

The Effects of Baptism
ACTIVITY AND DISCUSSION

Age Level: All ages

Recommended time: 10 minutes

What you need: The Effects of Baptism (**page 32** in the children's activity book)

What you need to know before you begin:

Baptism is a visible sign that effects what it signifies, as given to us directly by Christ. In Baptism, the baptized are:

> Forgiven of all sin, and the gifts of the Holy Spirit are infused into their souls.

> Reborn into new life in Christ. This means they are made new creatures in the sight of God and part of His family, making them co-heirs to all God's promises.

> Made members of the Body of Christ and temples of the Holy Spirit. This allows them access to all the other Sacraments and allows them to share in the priesthood of Christ, taking up Christ's mission to share the Gospel and make disciples.

> Given an indelible spiritual mark on their soul. No sin can remove this seal from the soul. It marks him forever as belonging to God, set apart for the day of redemption and eternal life with Him (see CCC 1279-1280).

Activity

A. Have your older children turn to **The Effects of Baptism (page 32 in the children's activity book)**. Ask them to read the *Catechism* quotes on the worksheet and write each of them in their own words.

B. As your older children work through the activity, explain the effects of Baptism to your younger children in a way they will understand. Make sure to explain all of the effects: forgiveness of sins, rebirth in Christ, being made members of the Church, and given an indelible spiritual mark.

BONUS ACTIVITY
Baptism SketchPad video

Age Level: All ages
Recommended time: 6 minutes
What you need: Sophia SketchPad Baptism video, found at **SophiaSketchPad.org**

Together, watch the six-minute Sophia SketchPad video on Baptism. The free video is available at **SophiaSketchPad.org**. Ask your children what they thought the most interesting part of the video was.

ACTIVITY 4

Remembering Your Baptism
DISCUSSION AND ACTIVITY

Age Level: All ages

Recommended time: 10-15 minutes

What you need: Baptismal Remembrance (**page 33** in the children's activity book), family photos, baptismal sign keepsakes

What you need to know before you begin:

At each Baptism, there are several visible signs that point to these invisible realities:

> **Water**, which is part of the essential rite of Baptism, symbolizes death, purification, regeneration, and renewal.

> **The candle**, lit from the Easter candle, symbolizes how Christ has enlightened the baptized.

> **The white garment** symbolizes that the baptized person has put on Christ, and has risen with Christ.

> **Oil** symbolizes the gift of the Holy Spirit to the new Christian, who is annointed priest, prophet, and king.

Activity

A. Explain to your children that Sacraments have matter and form. The matter is the physical material used. The form refers to the words that are spoken. In the Sacrament's most fundamental form, the minister of Baptism (ordinarily a priest) immerses the person being baptized three times in water (or pours water three times upon his head) while saying the words given to us by Jesus, "I baptize you in the name of the Father, and of the Son, and of the Holy Spirit" (see Matthew 28:19).

B. Then have children turn to **Baptismal Remembrance (page 33 in the children's activity book)**. Work individually with each of your children to fill in the information about their Baptisms. Discuss how God placed an indelible spiritual mark on their souls that marked them forever as belonging to God. They were set apart for eternal life with Him. Your children's Baptism days were the most important days of their lives!

C. Tell them stories of any special or memorable things that happened at their Baptisms and show them photos, if you have any. Then go over the visible signs of Baptism (water, candle, white garment, oils), explain how each was used at their Baptisms, and explain what they signify. If you kept any of these items (like the candle or the white garment), you may want to get them out to do a show-and-tell as you go over the signs.

ACTIVITY 5

Jesus' Baptism
SCRIPTURE AND SACRED ART ACTIVITY

Age Level: All ages
Recommended time: 10 minutes
What you need: Bible, Jesus' Baptism (**page 34** in the children's activity book), markers and/or crayons

Activity

A. Show your children the art on the following page while you read aloud the story of the Baptism of Jesus from Matthew 3:13-17:

> Then Jesus came from Galilee to John at the Jordan to be baptized by him.
>
> John tried to prevent him, saying, "I need to be baptized by you, and yet you are coming to me?"
>
> Jesus said to him in reply, "Allow it now, for thus it is fitting for us to fulfill all righteousness." Then he allowed him.
>
> After Jesus was baptized, he came up from the water and behold, the heavens were opened [for him], and he saw the Spirit of God descending like a dove [and] coming upon him. And a voice came from the heavens, saying, "This is my beloved Son, with whom I am well pleased."

B. Explain that in this picture we see what happened when Jesus was baptized: the Holy Spirit descended in the form of a dove, and the Father's voice was heard. The Father told everyone that He was pleased with His Son Jesus. Though we cannot see it, the same thing happens every time a person is baptized.

C. Have younger children turn to **Jesus' Baptism (page 34 in the children's activity book)**, and while they complete the coloring page, explain that Jesus was without sin and did not need to be baptized. But He allowed His cousin John to baptize Him to teach us how to be holy and to show us the way to salvation.

The Baptism of Christ, by Antoine Coypel.

 Connection to the Catechism

Our Lord voluntarily submitted himself to the baptism of St. John, intended for sinners, in order to fulfill all righteousness. (CCC 1224)

Baptismal Garment
GRACE PERSON ACTIVITY

Age Level: All ages

Recommended time: 10 minutes

What you need: Baptismal Garment Template (**page 35** in the children's activity book), scissors

Activity

A. Before you begin, read aloud to your children John 13:5-8:

> Then [Jesus] poured water into a basin and began to wash the disciples' feet and dry them with the towel around his waist. He came to Simon Peter, who said to him, "Master, are you going to wash my feet?"
>
> Jesus answered and said to him, "What I am doing, you do not understand now, but you will understand later."
>
> Peter said to him, "You will never wash my feet."
>
> Jesus answered him, "Unless I wash you, you will have no inheritance with me."

B. Focus your children on Jesus' words to St. Peter: "Unless I wash you, you will have no inheritance with me."

C. Ask your children: "What is an inheritance? Who normally receives an inheritance?" The answer is that, ordinarily, a child inherits things from his parents. Remember that Jesus is God. We become God's children in Baptism. When Jesus washes the feet of the Apostles, it reminds us of how He cleanses us in Baptism! This is why we receive a white garment when we are baptized. The garment is a sign that we have "put on Christ," who is pure and sinless.

D. Next, ask your children: "What inheritance do we receive from Him when He washes us?" The grace we receive in Baptism makes us more like our Heavenly Father, and the home He offers us is Heaven. We might squander it, like any inheritance, if we choose to reject His love. This is why it's so important to pray always and to receive the Sacraments!

E. After you have completed this Scripture reflection, have each family member tear out **Baptismal Garment Template (page 35 in the children's activity book)** and cut out the garment. If you wish, decorate it with white fabric, lace, or ribbon, then have each person place it on your Grace Person.

 ### Connection to the Catechism

The white garment symbolizes that the person baptized has put on Christ, has risen with Christ. (CCC 1243)

St. Catherine of Alexandria
SAINT OF THE MONTH

Age Level: All ages
Recommended time: 10 minutes
What you need: St. Catherine of Alexandria (**page 36** in the children's activity book), markers and/or crayons

Activity

Read aloud the story of this month's saint. You may also want to show them the full page saint image. While you are reading or sometime the next day, have them complete the coloring page on **page 37** of the children's activity book.

Biography of St. Catherine of Alexandria

CATHERINE was born in the year 287 in Alexandria, Egypt. When she was young, she read and studied as much as she could. She had a vision of Jesus and Mary, and she became a Christian. This was brave because in the time and place Catherine lived, being a Christian was illegal. The penalty was often torture and death!

But Catherine was not afraid. Since she was the governor's daughter, she could talk to the Roman emperor, Maxentius. She told the emperor to stop being cruel to Christians. The emperor brought 50 people to debate with Catherine. But Catherine was a very good speaker. She not only won the debate, but even won more than 200 converts, including members of Maxentius's own family. The emperor was very angry. He had the new Christians put to death, and he threw Catherine in jail.

Even in prison, St. Catherine gave every moment to Christ. Many people came to visit her, including the emperor's wife. Many of these people became Christians after their meetings with Catherine. The emperor had them all killed.

When the emperor saw that torture and imprisonment did not stop Catherine from speaking the truth about Jesus Christ, he tried something new. He offered to marry her if she would deny the Catholic Faith. She refused. Catherine told him, "I have become a bride of Christ." So the emperor sentenced Catherine to death. She was 18 years old.

St. Catherine of Alexandria is a great example of courage. She is the patron saint of philosophers, preachers, and young female students. Her feast day is November 25.

BAPTISM
The Gateway to Life in the Spirit

November in Review

THIS MONTH YOU EXPLORED AS A FAMILY THE QUESTIONS:

How did I become a part of God's family?

Why was I baptized?

What happens during a Baptism?

In Lesson 3 your children learned:

- The Sacraments of Initiation make us members of the Church, strengthen us for our life's journey, and give us our vocation as Christians.
- We are all called to be holy and to evangelize.

In Lesson 4 your children learned:

- Baptism is the gateway to the Christian life, and is necessary for salvation.
- The Sacrament of Baptism is pre-figured in the Old Testament.
- In Baptism our sins are forgiven, we are reborn in Christ and made sons and daughters of God, made members of the Church, and receive an indelible mark on our souls.

In this space below, write some reflections about the past month. What was your favorite activity? What didn't go as well? Will you adjust anything about what you're doing? What special intentions do you have for next month?

December
OVERVIEW

VERSE OF THE MONTH

ACTS 8:17

Then they laid hands on them and they received the Holy Spirit.

SAINT OF THE MONTH

ST. STEPHEN

LESSON 5

CONFIRMATION

Overview

Confirmation is often misunderstood as a kind of "graduation" or public acceptance of the Faith. In fact, the Sacrament of Confirmation is an important step on the path of Christian initiation that completes, or confirms, the outpouring of the Holy Spirit received at Baptism and sends the person out to proclaim boldly the Good News.

Catechism Articles to Read

> 1285-1321

Words to Know

> Anoint
> Apostle
> Confirmation
> Holy Spirit
> Pentecost
> Gifts of the Holy Spirit

BY THE END OF THIS MONTH, YOUR CHILDREN SHOULD BE ABLE TO:

✓ Recite this month's Scripture Memorization

✓ Define this month's Words to Know

✓ Describe who the Apostles were, what their mission was, and how all Christians share in that mission

✓ Understand what Confirmation is and how it affects us

✓ Tell you about St. Stephen

YOUR
Catholic Home
SPIRITUAL READING

We learn this month about the seven gifts of the Holy Spirit. Like all of God's gifts of grace, the gifts of the Holy Spirit will bear fruit in our lives only if we respond with prayer and take time to develop them. One great way we can strive to nurture and grow the gifts of the Holy Spirit is through spiritual reading.

Practice It!

This month, add books of spiritual reading to your prayer space. Daily meditations are usually short and digestible, making it easy to commit to reading one meditation a day. Depending on the books you choose, each family member could read them independently, or you could read aloud from one book every evening or before leaving the house each morning. Be sure to share with each other the new understandings you have received from God through your spiritual reading!

Celebrate!

ST. STEPHEN
DECEMBER 26

Now Stephen, filled with grace and power, was working great wonders and signs among the people.
—Acts 6:8

THINGS TO DO THIS MONTH:

1 Add a book of spiritual reading to your prayer corner.

2 Observe the season in your home with an Advent wreath.

VERSE OF THE MONTH
ACTS 8:17

Then they laid hands on them and they received the Holy Spirit.

REMEMBER!
The seven gifts of the Holy Spirit are wisdom, understanding, counsel, fortitude, knowledge, piety, and fear of the Lord.

MEMORIZE!

Confirmation completes, or confirms, the outpouring of the Holy Spirit received at Baptism and sends the person out to proclaim boldly the Good News.

ST. STEPHEN

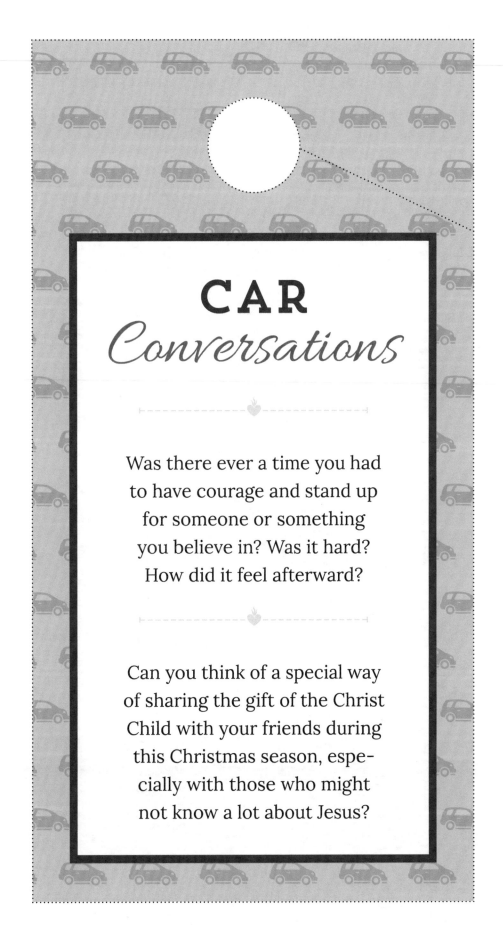

CAR
Conversations

Was there ever a time you had to have courage and stand up for someone or something you believe in? Was it hard? How did it feel afterward?

Can you think of a special way of sharing the gift of the Christ Child with your friends during this Christmas season, especially with those who might not know a lot about Jesus?

LESSON 5

CONFIRMATION

Activities and Key Concepts

Activities you will do with your children	Key concepts the activity will teach	Recommended age and time
Marking something as Our Own Family discussion	Confirmation places an indelible mark on our souls.	**Ages:** All ages **Time:** 10 minutes
Confirmation Prefigured Discussion and Scripture reading	Old Testament priests and kings were anointed with holy oil as a symbol of consecration.	**Ages:** All ages **Time:** 10 minutes
What Is Confirmation? Reading and discussion	Confirmation increases the gifts of the Holy Spirit within the person and gives the person special strength to live out the Christian mission.	**Ages:** All ages **Time:** 10 minutes
Ascension and Pentecost Scripture reading and creative activity	When we are confirmed, we receive an outpouring of the Holy Spirit like the Apostles received at Pentecost.	**Ages:** Ages 5-8 **Time:** 5 minutes
Gifts of the Holy Spirit Family discussion	Confirmation increases in us the gifts of the Holy Spirit	**Ages:** Ages 8 and up **Time:** 5 minutes
I Belong to Jesus Grace person activity	Review of the rite of Confirmation.	**Ages:** All ages **Time:** 5 minutes

LESSON 5
WORDS TO KNOW

The Words to Know are words that you and your children should know and understand at the end of this month. Use your best judgment about which words to expect each of your children to learn. For older children, you may want to have them create flashcards to help them remember what they have learned.

Anoint	To rub something with holy oil.
Apostle	One of the twelve men chosen by Jesus to be the first priests.
Confirmation	A Sacrament on the path of Christian initiation that completes, or confirms, the outpouring of the Holy Spirit received at Baptism and sends the person out to proclaim boldly the Good News.
Holy Spirit	The third Divine Person of the Blessed Trinity.
Pentecost	The "birthday of the Church," when Jesus sent the Holy Spirit to Mary and the Apostles.
Gifts of the Holy Spirit	Gifts that are increased in us in the Sacrament of Confirmation: wisdom, understanding, counsel, knowledge, fortitude, piety, and fear of the Lord.

Please choose from the activities for the month.

It is not necessary to complete every activity. We offer a wealth of activities to choose from because each child learns differently, so select the activities that best suit the learning needs of you family. Feel free to shorten or improvise on each activity as necessary. You know best what your family needs!

ACTIVITY 1

Marking Something as Our Own
FAMILY DISCUSSION

Age Level: All ages
Recommended time: 10 minutes

Discussion with Older Children

A. Ask your children, "How do you know something is yours?" Ask them for specific examples: Perhaps your favorite jeans or shoes are broken in just right, your favorite baseball glove fits your hand perfectly from use, or maybe you've marked or changed something somehow to make it yours.

B. Now ask, what are some steps you've taken to make sure that others know this thing belongs to you? Maybe you've written your name on it; cars have license plates; certain types of merchandise have serial numbers that can be recorded, and so forth.

C. Transition the conversation to non-material things. Ask your children to whom or what do they belong. They may say that they belong to their parents, or to themselves, to clubs or groups, or to God. Then brainstorm some outward signs of those memberships. These may range from the external and temporary (membership cards, T-shirts, pins) to the more permanent (wedding rings, tribal tattoos, branding, and so forth).

D. Explain that the Sacrament of Confirmation is a way in which the Father seals us with the Holy Spirit, or seals us as His. He also consecrates us (sets us apart), commissions us, enrolls us in His service forever, and promises us His help in trials (CCC 1296).

Discussion with Younger Children

A. Ask your younger children to bring you a favorite toy or any other special item that means a lot to them. Ask them to show you how they know this item belongs to them.

B. Talk about how you know that each of your children belongs to you because you welcomed him or her into your family with a baby shower and gave birth to or adopted him or her. If possible, point out the similarities in your appearance. Maybe you have the same eye color or the same nose. With a hug, tell your child that you will always be his or her parent, no matter what. Nothing can change that.

C. Transition the discussion to how much God loves each of us, and how He marks us as belonging to Him in Baptism and Confirmation. Confirmation places an indelible (permanent) seal on our souls! We cannot see it, but it is real. And this seal lasts forever. Nothing can change it. We belong to God forever, and He loves us forever.

 Connection to the Catechism

By the sacrament of Confirmation, [the baptized] are more perfectly bound to the Church and are enriched with a special strength of the Holy Spirit. Hence they are, as true witnesses of Christ, more strictly obliged to spread and defend the faith by word and deed. (CCC 1285)

BONUS ACTIVITY
Confirmation SketchPad Video

Age Level: All ages

Recommended time: 6 minutes

What you will need: Sophia SketchPad Confirmation video, found at **SophiaSketchPad.org**

Together, watch the six-minute Sophia SketchPad video on Confirmation. The free video is available at **SophiaSketchPad.org**. When you are finished watching, ask your children if anything in the video surprised them.

ACTIVITY 2

Confirmation Prefigured
DISCUSSION AND SCRIPTURE READING

Age Level: All ages

Recommended time: 10 minutes

What you need: Bible

Anointing of David, by Paolo Veronese.

What you need to know before you begin:

The roots of the Sacrament of Confirmation can be found throughout the Old Testament. From early on, God made known to His people what He desired for them: "You will be to me a kingdom of priests, a holy nation" (Exodus 19:6). God sought to make of His people a royal priesthood who would proclaim and glorify His name to all the nations and serve Him in love.

By the time Israel became a royal kingdom, it was already well established that priests and kings were anointed with holy oil as a symbol of consecration—that is, of being set apart as belonging to God—and as a symbol of the outpouring of God's Spirit upon them to commission them for God's service and to strengthen them for the work ahead according to their position. All of the kings in the line of David were anointed at their inauguration as king and became "messiahs" in Hebrew or "christs" in Greek, both of which mean "anointed one." Later, the prophets foretold of a day on which God would "pour out [His] spirit upon all flesh" (Joel 2:28).

Jesus, while completing His work of salvation, announced, "For on [the Son of Man] the Father, God, has set His seal" (John 6:27), proclaiming that He was the awaited Christ. Further, He promised to send the Holy Spirit, the Advocate, after Him to teach and to confirm all that has been revealed to us and to empower us to proclaim the Good News of salvation: "But you will receive power when the Holy Spirit comes upon you, and you will be my witnesses in Jerusalem, throughout Judea and Samaria, and to the ends of the earth" (Acts 1:8). And on Pentecost, when the Blessed Virgin Mary and the Apostles had gathered in the Upper Room, with a rush of wind, the Holy Spirit descended upon them as tongues of fire and emboldened them to preach to the gathered crowd and soon to all the nations.

Discussion

A. Discuss the information with your children at a level they will understand, making sure to cover the following points:

> God has always desired for His people to be a "royal priesthood," anointed and consecrated (or set apart in a sacred way) as His Chosen People.

> The Sacrament of Confirmation completes the work begun in us at our Baptism and sets us apart as this very royal priesthood proclaimed since the Old Testament.

> In Confirmation, we receive an outpouring of the Holy Spirit that empowers us, like the Apostles at Pentecost, to proclaim the Good News of Jesus Christ and make disciples of all the nations.

B. Read aloud Leviticus 8:6-13 while your children follow along.

Bringing forward Aaron and his sons, Moses first washed them with water. Then he put the tunic on Aaron, girded him with the sash, clothed him with the robe, placed the ephod on him, and girded him with the ephod's embroidered belt, fastening the ephod on him with it. He then set the breastpiece on him, putting the Urim and Thummim in it. He put the turban on his head, attaching the gold medallion, the sacred headband, on the front of the turban, as the LORD had commanded Moses to do.

Taking the anointing oil, Moses anointed and consecrated the tabernacle and all that was in it. Then he sprinkled some of the oil seven times on the altar, and anointed the altar, with all its utensils, and the laver, with its base, to consecrate them. He also poured some of the anointing oil on Aaron's head and anointed him, to consecrate him.

Moses likewise brought forward Aaron's sons, clothed them with tunics, girded them with sashes, and put skullcaps on them, as the LORD had commanded him to do.

C. Explain that this passage describes how Moses anointed the first Levitical priests of the Old Testament: Aaron and his sons. Ask your children what we see Moses do in this passage to anoint Aaron and his sons as priests.

> First, he washes them with water.

> Then he clothes them with all of the signs of their position.

> Last, he pours oil over them to set them apart for God and anoint them with God's Spirit.

D. Ask your children if they see how what Moses does is similar to both Baptism and Confirmation.

> Moses first washes Aaron and his sons with water, as we are cleansed by the water of Baptism.

> Then he anoints them with oil to complete the outpouring of God's Spirit, which we receive when we are anointed in Confirmation.

 Connection to the Catechism

In the Old Testament the prophets announced that the Spirit of the Lord would rest on the hoped-for Messiah for his saving mission. (CCC 1286)

BONUS ACTIVITY
Confirmation Prefigured Scripture Search

Age Level: Older children

Recommended time: 15-20 minutes

What you will need: Bible, Confirmation Prefigured (**page 41** in the children's activity book)

Have your older children turn to **Confirmation Prefigured (page 41 in the children's activity book)** and read the information to reinforce what you talked about in the Confirmation Prefigured Discussion. Then, have them use their Bibles to complete the chart.

1. **Genesis 2:7:** God breathes His Spirit into Adam./ He is given life by the Spirit.

2. **1 Samuel 16:13:** The Spirit rushes upon David after his anointing./ David is made king.

3. **Ezekiel 36:26-27:** The Spirit is put within us./ The Spirit allows us to keep God's commands.

4. **Joel 3:1-2:** The Spirit will be poured out upon us./ There will be prophesy, dreams, and visions.

5. **Isaiah 11:2:** The Spirit will rest upon him./ The Spirit will give him counsel, knowledge, and strength.

6. **Isaiah 61:1:** The Spirit has anointed him./ The Spirit has sent him to bring good new to the afflicted.

What is Confirmation?
READING AND DISCUSSION

Age Level: All ages

Recommended time: 10 minutes

What you will need: What Is Confirmation? (**page 43** in the children's activity book)

Activity

A. Read the essay on "What is Confirmation?" below.

B. Discuss the essay as a family. For younger children, go over the main points at a level that they will understand. For older children, you may have them read the essay themselves, then discuss with them what they read. The essay is also in the children's activity book on **page 43.**

C. Make sure to discuss the following points:

> The recipient of Confirmation (the confirmand) must be a baptized person. If he has reached the age of reason, he must be in a state of grace, profess the faith, have the intention of receiving the Sacrament, and be prepared to be a disciple of Christ.

> Confirmation is an outpouring of the Holy Spirit on the confirmand.

> The bishop is the ordinary minister of the Sacrament, and to confer the Sacrament, he speaks the words "Be sealed with the gift of the Holy Spirit" while laying his hands on the confirmand.

What is Confirmation? Essay

The Sacrament of Confirmation is often misunderstood, despite the rich history of the Sacrament that reaches back to Jesus and the Apostles and its deep roots in the Old Testament. Contrary to popular belief, it is not a graduation ceremony

Holy Spirit at Pentecost stained glass window, Saint James the Greater Catholic Church.

or the Catholic equivalent of a Jewish bar mitzvah. Rather, the Sacrament of Confirmation is an important step on the path of Christian initiation that completes, or confirms, the outpouring of the Holy Spirit received at Baptism and sends the person out to proclaim boldly the Good News. "By the sacrament of Confirmation, [the baptized] are more perfectly bound to the Church and are enriched with a special strength of the Holy Spirit. Hence they are, as true witnesses of Christ, more strictly obliged to spread and defend the faith by word and deed" (CCC 1285).

"Be Sealed with the Gift of the Holy Spirit"

The tradition of anointing with holy oil, or chrism, as a seal of the Holy Spirit continues in the Sacrament of Confirmation. The bishop, the ordinary minister of the Sacrament, speaks the words "Be sealed with the gift of the Holy Spirit" while laying his hands on the confirmand, signifying the outpouring of the Spirit in a succession of imposition of hands that stretches back to the Apostles. These words and actions bring to fruition God's desire for His people to be a royal priesthood. Indeed, Confirmation increases the gifts of the Holy Spirit within the person, and "gives [him] a special strength of the Holy Spirit to spread and defend the faith by word and action as true witnesses of Christ, to confess the name of Christ boldly, and never to be ashamed of the Cross" (CCC 1303).

The Sacrament of Confirmation uniquely gives us the fullness of the Christian mission as well as the ability and strength to complete it. In Confirmation we, as St. Paul proclaims, "put on the armor of God" and "hold faith as a shield, to quench all [the] flaming arrows of the evil one" (Ephesians 6:11, 16).

Who Can Receive Confirmation?

The Church teaches clearly that "Every baptized person not yet confirmed can and should receive the sacrament of Confirmation" (CCC 1306). In the early Church, Baptism and Confirmation were received together. Increasing numbers of infant Baptisms made it impossible for the bishop to be present for all of them, and for this and other reasons, the two began to be offered separately. In the Latin rite today, Confirmation is most commonly received after the recipient has attained the age of reason, with the age being set by the bishop. The Eastern Church, on the other hand, retained the tradition of offering Confirmation at the same time as Baptism. In this way, the Eastern Church emphasizes the unity of Baptism and Confirmation.

To receive Confirmation, a baptized person "must profess the faith, be in the state of grace, have the intention of receiving the Sacrament, and be prepared to assume the role of disciple and witness to Christ," both in the Church and in the world (CCC 1319). A candidate for Confirmation should seek a practicing Catholic to serve as a sponsor, to be a model of faith and encouragement. Because of Confirmation's close connection to Baptism, it is desirable, if possible, that one of the baptismal godparents serve as the sponsor. It is also customary that the one to be confirmed chooses the name of a saint – someone who exemplifies to them a life of holiness – as a Confirmation name.

ACTIVITY 4

Ascension and Pentecost
SCRIPTURE READING AND CREATIVE ACTIVITY

Age Level: Ages 5-8

Recommended time: 5-10 minutes

What you will need: Ascension and Pentecost (**page 45** in the children's activity book), markers and/or crayons

Ascension, by John Singleton Copley .

What you need to know before you begin:

When we are confirmed, we receive an outpouring of the Holy Spirit like the Apostles received at Pentecost.

Activity

A. Before beginning this activity, explain to your children that at the Ascension, Jesus commanded His disciples to preach the Good News and to baptize believers in the name of the Father and of the Son, and of the Holy Spirit. He promised to send the Holy Spirit to help them do this.

B. Have your children turn to **Ascension and Pentecost (page 45 in the children's activity book)**. While you read Acts 1:8 aloud, have them color the picture:

> [Y]ou will receive power when the Holy Spirit comes upon you, and you will be my witnesses in Jerusalem, throughout Judea and Samaria, and to the ends of the earth.

C. Next, set the scene of what led up to Pentecost: the Apostles were hiding in the Upper Room. They had given their lives to Jesus and had been taught by Him for three years, but they were too afraid to fulfill the mission He had given them.

D. Now read the account of the descent of the Holy Spirit upon the Apostles at Pentecost in Acts 2:1-15 while your children color the picture of Pentecost:

> When the time for Pentecost was fulfilled, they were all in one place together. And suddenly there came from the sky a noise like a strong driving wind, and it filled the entire house in which they were. Then there appeared to them tongues as of fire, which parted and came to rest on each one of them. And they were all filled with the holy Spirit and began to speak in different tongues, as the Spirit enabled them to proclaim.

E. Remind your children that earlier, St. Peter had denied that he even knew Jesus! But after he received the Holy Spirit, he boldly proclaimed the truth. Three thousand people were baptized on that day alone! On the day of Pentecost the Church was born through the power of the Holy Spirit. It is that same Spirit who still lives in the Church today, empowering all who receive Him in the Sacrament of Confirmation to continue to spread the Kingdom of God in word and deed.

F. Help your children complete the activity by answering the questions together.

Answers:

1. The Holy Spirit
2. To be His witnesses
3. Someone who gives testimony, or tells others what he saw (witnessed)
4. A strong driving wind
5. Tongues of fire
6. The Holy Spirit
7. Proclaim Jesus in many different languages

BONUS ACTIVITY
Picturing Confirmation

Age Level: All ages

Recommended time: 10 minutes

What you will need: Picturing Confirmation (**page 48** in the children's activity book)

Read aloud all of the Scripture verses, or have your older children read them independently. Have your children choose one and use their imagination to draw a creative scene that represents the verse. Discuss with them how, just as soldiers would wear their king's seal and armor into battle, Confirmation seals us for Christ and gives us His spiritual protection.

 Connection to the Catechism

Confirmation ... in a certain way perpetuates the grace of Pentecost in the Church. (CCC 1288)

Gifts of the Holy Spirit
FAMILY DISCUSSION

Age Level: Ages 8 and up
Recommended time: 5 minutes

What you need to know before you begin:

The effect of the Sacrament of Confirmation is a "full outpouring of the Holy Spirit as once granted to the apostles on the day of Pentecost" (CCC 1302). Confirmation increases the grace given to us at Baptism and increases in us the gifts of the Holy Spirit:

> **Wisdom:** Wisdom allows us to know the purpose and plan of God and value it above all else. God's wisdom is His truth. God gives us a share in His wisdom to allow us to recognize the truth and see things from His point of view.

> **Understanding:** Understanding empowers human intelligence to know and comprehend those truths of the Catholic Faith that go beyond human reasoning. It allows us to discover God's will in everything through prayer, reading Scripture, and receiving the Sacraments.

> **Counsel:** Counsel, or right judgment, helps us to know right from wrong and to avoid sin. It allows us to make the right decisions in the face of temptation and evil. Right judgment empowers us to live a moral life and attain salvation.

> **Fortitude:** Fortitude emboldens us to stand up for and defend the Catholic Faith in the face of persecution, even to the point of enduring physical harm or death. This gift strengthens us to do God's will in our lives and helps us to overcome our fear.

> **Knowledge:** Knowledge allows us to be aware of God's plan in our lives and to apply it and take action on it. Knowledge sheds light on our weaknesses, sins, and failures and helps us strive to overcome them with the grace of God.

> **Piety:** Piety, or reverence, moves us to serve God in humility and love. It allows us to worship Him rightly, not because we feel a responsibility or duty, but because we love Him and desire to worship Him.

> **Fear of the Lord:** The gift of fear of the Lord, sometimes called awe, allows us to recognize that God is God and we are not. By this gift, we rightly know our relationship to God and His glory and greatness. We fear displeasing God by our sin and desire to be close to Him.

Discussion

A. Talk with your older children about each of the Gifts of the Holy Spirit. To reinforce this teaching, read aloud from Isaiah 11:2:

The spirit of the LORD shall rest upon him: a spirit of wisdom and of understanding, a spirit of counsel and of strength, a spirit of knowledge and of fear of the LORD.

B. Explain that, as with all of God's gifts of grace, our free response to them determines whether they will bear fruit. A person who has just been confirmed does not instantly become wise, strong, and so forth. Rather, God gives us the seeds of these virtues, and it's up to us to develop them through prayer and discipline. Over time, we will find ourselves responding to the Holy Spirit's promptings more naturally as those virtues bear fruit. What are the fruits of the Spirit? The Bible tells us: "[T]he fruit of the Spirit is love, joy, peace, patience, kindness, generosity, faithfulness, gentleness, self-control" (Galatians 5:22-23).

 Connection to the Catechism

Confirmation ... increases the gifts of the Holy Spirit in us. (CCC 1303)

ACTIVITY 6

I Belong to Jesus
GRACE PERSON ACTIVITY

Age Level: All ages

Recommended time: 5 minutes

What you need: I Belong to Jesus (**page 49** in the children's activity book)

Activity

This month you will "seal" your Grace Person "with the gift of the Holy Spirit."

A. First, have your children turn to **I Belong to Jesus (page 49 in the children's activity book)**. Ask them to look at and color the picture of a person receiving the Sacrament of Confirmation. Point out that, no matter what the age of the person being confirmed, the bishop anoints his or her forehead with holy oil (also called chrism), lays his hand on him or her, and says, "Be sealed with the gift of the Holy Spirit."

B. Explain to your children that the holy oil is oil mixed with balsam that is consecrated by the bishop at the Chrism Mass on the morning of Holy Thursday. If you have ever smelled it, let them know how wonderful and "holy" it smells! Then have your children color the seal the color of holy oil (or chrism).

C. Finally, have one child cut out the seal and, while everyone gathers to watch, place it on the forehead of your Grace Person, while saying what the bishop says: "Be sealed with the Gift of the Holy Spirit."

D. This would be a good time to ask your older children to recall the gifts of the Holy Spirit from their Words to Know, and/or to ask your older children to recall Isaiah 11:2: "The spirit of the LORD shall rest upon him: a spirit of wisdom and of understanding, a spirit of counsel and of strength, a spirit of knowledge and of fear of the LORD."

E. You might also explain to your children why the Sacrament of Confirmation can be received only once — because it places an indelible (or permanent) mark on the soul.

St. Stephen
SAINT OF THE MONTH

Age Level: All ages

Recommended time: 10 minutes

What you need: St. Stephen (**page 51** in the children's activity book)

Activity

Read aloud the story of this month's saint to your children. You may also want to show them the full page saint image. While you are reading or sometime the next day, have them complete the coloring page on **page 52** in the children's activity book.

Biography of St. Stephen

STEPHEN was a Jewish man who became one of the first Christians. He was full of wisdom and faith from the Holy Spirit. The disciples of Jesus ordained him a deacon. He had the task of taking care of widows who became Christian. The Bible also tells us that Stephen worked miracles and that he was full of grace and power.

Some Jewish men who hated Christianity tried to argue with Stephen, but they could not outsmart the wisdom he received from the Holy Spirit. They were so angry that they bribed other men to falsely accuse Stephen of telling lies about the Old Testament prophet Moses.

On these false accusations, Stephen was brought to the Jewish court. He defended himself by telling the story of Moses. Moses saved the Israelites from the pagan Egyptians. But the Israelites betrayed Moses and God by worshipping a pagan idol. Stephen told the Jewish men that, like Moses, every Old Testament prophet was betrayed and persecuted by the Jews, even though the prophets tried to tell the Jewish people about Jesus. When Jesus came, He was also betrayed, persecuted, and killed by Jewish people, including by the men who arrested Stephen.

Then the Jewish men were filled with rage because they did not want to hear the truth. Stephen looked up, and he saw Heaven, with Jesus standing at the right of God the Father. Stephen told the men what he saw, but they refused to listen. They dragged him out of the city and threw stones at him. Just before he died, Stephen prayed that Jesus would be merciful to the men who were killing him. A martyr is someone who is killed for his or her religious faith. St. Stephen was the first martyr of the Church. His life shows us what it means to live out all seven gifts of the Holy Spirit.

December in Review

THIS MONTH YOU EXPLORED AS A FAMILY THE QUESTIONS:

What is Confirmation?

What are its effects?

In Lesson 5 your children learned:

- ‣ Confirmation places an indelible mark on our souls.
- ‣ Confirmation is prefigured in the Old Testament anointing of priests and kings.
- ‣ Confirmation increases the gifts of the Holy Spirit in us, and gives us special strength to spread and defend the Faith.

In this space below, write some reflections about the past month. What was your favorite activity? What didn't go as well? Will you adjust anything about what you're doing? What special intentions do you have for next month?

January

OVERVIEW

VERSES OF THE MONTH
1 CORINTHIANS 5:7
JOHN 6:51

SAINT OF THE MONTH
ST. THOMAS AQUINAS

LESSON 6

THE EUCHARIST: JESUS, THE PASSOVER LAMB

Overview

This lesson examines the Eucharist as a sacrifice, and its foreshadowing in the Old Testament—especially as seen in the Passover. In the Old Covenant, God saved the physical lives of His people, the Israelites, through the blood of a lamb. In the New Covenant, Jesus saves the spiritual lives of His people through the shedding of His own Blood. It is this sacrifice of Jesus' Body and Blood that we commemorate every time we celebrate the Eucharist at Holy Mass.

Catechism Articles to Read

> 1322-1419

Words to Know

> Covenant
> Eucharist
> Passover
> *Pascha*
> Paschal Lamb

LESSON 7

HOLY MASS AND THE EFFECTS OF THE EUCHARIST

Overview

This lesson examines the celebration of the Mass and how the gifts of bread and wine are transformed in the Body and Blood of Jesus. When we receive Holy Communion, our souls are strengthened, our venial sins forgiven, and we are united with other Christians in the Body of Christ. Only Catholics in a state of grace should receive Communion in order to receive Jesus' Body and Blood worthily. We should receive Holy Communion reverently and often.

Catechism Articles to Read

> 1335-1355

Words to Know

> Altar

> Tabernacle

> Transubstantiation

BY THE END OF THIS MONTH, YOUR CHILDREN SHOULD BE ABLE TO:

✓ Recite this month's Scripture Memorization

✓ Define this month's Words to Know

✓ Explain that Jesus Christ instituted the Eucharist at the Last Supper

✓ Understand that the Eucharist is the Body and Blood of Jesus Christ

✓ Explain some of the Old Testament roots of the Eucharist, and why Jesus is called the Paschal Lamb

✓ Tell you about St. Thomas Aquinas

YOUR
Catholic Home
SOLEMNITY OF MARY, MOTHER OF GOD

January 1 is the Solemnity of Mary, the Mother of God. A solemnity is a feast day of the highest rank. The Solemnity of Mary, the Mother of God is also a Holy Day of Obligation—a day when Catholics are required to attend Holy Mass.

Catholics honor the Virgin Mary for many reasons, such as her faith in God and her perfect obedience to His will. On January 1, we honor Mary's motherhood. Jesus has two natures—He is both fully God and fully man. Jesus existed with the Father from all eternity, but when He came down from Heaven and became man, He was conceived in Mary's womb by the Holy Spirit. Jesus is Mary's son: the Word made Flesh. Therefore it is fitting to say that Mary is the mother of God Incarnate: Jesus Christ.

Practice It!

Celebrate this solemnity by going to Mass as a family and adding a statue or icon of Mary to your prayer corner (or another prominent place in your home).

Celebrate!

ST. THOMAS AQUINAS
JANUARY 28

To love is to will the good of the other.
–St. Thomas Aquinas

THINGS TO DO THIS MONTH:

1 As a family, visit Jesus in the Blessed Sacrament.

2 Add a statue of Mary to your prayer corner.

REMEMBER!

"The holy Eucharist completes Christian initiation. Those who have been raised to the dignity of the royal priesthood by Baptism and configured more deeply to Christ by Confirmation participate with the whole community in the Lord's own sacrifice by means of the Eucharist" (1322).

VERSES OF THE MONTH

1 CORINTHIANS 5:7

For our paschal lamb, Christ, has been sacrificed.

JOHN 6:51

"I am the living bread that came down from heaven; whoever eats this bread will live forever; and the bread that I will give is my flesh for the life of the world."

MEMORIZE! The Eucharist is "the source and summit of the Christian life" (CCC 1324).

ST. THOMAS AQUINAS

SAINT OF THE MONTH

CAR
Conversations

Jesus waits for us in the Eucharist because He loves us and wants to be our friend. Sadly, there are many people who forget about Him, reject Him, or even disrespect Him.

Have you ever wanted to be friends with someone but he or she rejected you or even made fun of you? How did that make you feel?

Can you think of ways you can spend time with Jesus to comfort Him in place of all the people who have rejected Him?

LESSON 6

THE EUCHARIST: JESUS, THE PASSOVER LAMB

Activities and Key Concepts

Activities you will do with your children	Key concepts the activity will teach	Recommended age and time
What Is the Eucharist? Family discussion	The Eucharist is the source and summit of our Faith.	**Ages:** All ages **Time:** 15 minutes
The Passover Sacrifice Scripture search	The Eucharist is prefigured in the Passover.	**Ages:** Ages 8 and up **Time:** 10 minutes
Jesus, Our Passover Lamb Reflections and Booklet Scripture reflections and activity book	Jesus instituted the Eucharist at the Last Supper; Holy Mass re-presents the Last Supper.	**Ages:** All ages **Time:** 20 minutes
Old Covenant, New Covenant Matching activity	The New Covenant in Christ fulfills the Old Covenant.	**Ages:** All ages **Time:** 5 minutes

LESSON 6

WORDS TO KNOW

The Words to Know are words that you and your children should know and understand at the end of this month. Use your best judgment about which words to expect each of your children to learn. For older children, you may want to have them create flashcards to help them remember what they have learned.

Covenant	A promise that makes family bonds.
Eucharist	The Sacrament in which we receive Jesus Christ's Body and Blood at Holy Mass. The Eucharist completes Christian initiation.
Passover	The Jewish festival commemorating God's covenant with the Israelites, and how He saved them from slavery in Egypt.
Pascha	The Greek word for Passover.
Paschal Lamb	A title for Jesus that reminds us that His sacrifice saves us from sin.

Please choose from the activities for the month.

It is not necessary to complete every activity. We offer a wealth of activities to choose from because each child learns differently, so select the activities that best suit the learning needs of you family. Feel free to shorten or improvise on each activity as necessary. You know best what your family needs!

ACTIVITY 1

What Is the Eucharist?
FAMILY DISCUSSION

Age Level: All ages
Recommended time: 15 minutes

What you need to know before you begin:

Our study of the Sacraments of Initiation culminates in the Eucharist: "The holy Eucharist completes Christian initiation. Those who have been raised to the dignity of the royal priesthood by Baptism and configured more deeply to Christ by Confirmation participate with the whole community in the Lord's own sacrifice by means of the Eucharist" (CCC 1322).

The *Catechism of the Catholic Church* calls the Eucharist "the Sacrament of sacraments" (CCC 1330) and "the source and summit of the Christian life" (CCC 1324). All the other Sacraments and every ministry of the Church flow from the Eucharist and point us toward it. The reason for the centrality of the Eucharist is that the Eucharist is Christ Himself! In it, Christ offers for us his sacrifice of praise and thanksgiving to the Father, and through that sacrifice, the grace of salvation is poured out onto his Body, the Church.

The Last Supper, by Juan de Juanes.

Jesus instituted the Eucharist at the Last Supper. In anticipation of His Death on the Cross, Jesus gave His Apostles – whom He made the first priests – His Body and Blood to eat and drink. And because Jesus wanted all His people for all time to eat and drink of this heavenly food, He commanded them to continue to make present and real this Eucharistic sacrifice. "Do this in remembrance of me," Jesus instructed His Apostles. So whenever we celebrate Mass, we do so at Christ's command, and Jesus is made real and present to us.

Activity

A. Read aloud to your children from *Catechism of the Catholic Church* paragraph no. 1324:

> The Eucharist is "the source and summit of the Christian life."

B. Then ask them the following questions:

  › What is the source of a thing (like the source of a river)? *Where it comes from. Its origin or beginning.*

  › What is the summit of a thing (like the summit of a mountain)? *It's top or highest point.*

  › What do you think it means, then, to say that the Eucharist is the "source and summit of the Christian life"? *The Eucharist is where the Christian life comes from. It is the origin or beginning of the Christian life. The Eucharist is also where the Christian life flows from. The Eucharist is the peak or highest expression of the Christian life.*

C. Explain that the Eucharist is the Body and Blood of Jesus Christ. It is not just a symbol or a sign but His real Body and Blood, offered as a sacrifice of praise to God. Jesus instituted the Eucharist at the Last Supper, and because He wanted all His people for all time to eat and drink of this life-giving, heavenly food, He commanded them to continue to make present and real the Eucharistic sacrifice. So whenever we celebrate Mass, we do so at Christ's command, and Jesus is truly with us — Body, Blood, Soul, and Divinity.

 Connection to the Catechism

We carry out this command of the Lord by celebrating the memorial of his sacrifice. In so doing, we offer to the Father what he has himself given us: the gifts of his creation, bread and wine which, by the power of the Holy Spirit and by the words of Christ, have become the body and blood of Christ. Christ is thus really and mysteriously made present. (CCC 1357)

BONUS ACTIVITY
Pange Lingua prayer

Age Level: All ages
Recommended time: 5 minutes

Begin with the Sign of the Cross and pray a few verses of a prayer composed by St. Thomas Aquinas called the *Pange Lingua* (from its first lines, "Sing, my tongue the Savior's glory"). The last two verses of this prayer are usually sung at benediction (hymns sung before the Blessed Sacrament).

Sing, my tongue, the Savior's glory,
Of His Flesh, the mystery sing;
Of the Blood, all price exceeding,
Shed by our Immortal King,...
On the night of that Last Supper,
Seated with His chosen band,
He, the Paschal Victim eating,
First fulfills the Law's command;
Then as Food to all His brethren
Gives Himself with His own Hand.
Word-made-Flesh, the bread of nature
By His Word to Flesh He turns;
Wine into His Blood He changes:
What though sense no change discerns.
Amen. Alleluia.

ACTIVITY 2

The Passover Sacrifice
SCRIPTURE SEARCH

Age Level: Ages 8 and up

Recommended time: 10 minutes

What you need: Bible, Passover Sacrifice (**page 56** in the children's activity book)

And There Was A Great Cry In Egypt, by Arthur Hacker.

What you need to know before you begin:

The Eucharist has deep and mysterious roots in the Old Testament, conveyed by events, archetypes, and symbols all guided by the hand of Divine Providence. The most significant of these is the Passover. The Passover was the principal Jewish feast of the Old Testament. It was instituted to commemorate the Jews' liberation from Egyptian slavery and the fulfillment of God's promise to Abraham that He would establish a people uniquely His. God's people were commanded to recall this saving event for all generations and to keep this feast day forever.

To deliver His Chosen People from slavery, God sent a series of plagues to Egypt. The last of these was to kill every firstborn son throughout the land. God told the Israelites to sacrifice a lamb according to specific instructions and to apply its blood to the doorposts and lintels of their homes as a sign for God to pass over their homes and spare their firstborn. "The blood will be a sign for you on the houses where you are; and when I see the blood, I will pass over you" (Exodus 12:13). God also commanded the Israelites to eat the lamb: "They will consume its meat that same night, eating it roasted with unleavened bread and bitter herbs" (Exodus 12:8-9). Finally, God also commanded the Israelites to remember this great act of His salvation by holding a yearly festival known as the Passover: "This day will be a day of remembrance for you, which your future generations will celebrate with pilgrimage to the LORD; you will celebrate it as a statute forever" (Exodus 12:14).

Many centuries later, it was precisely at the Passover meal when Jesus instituted a New and everlasting Covenant and gave His friends the greatest gift of all — His Body and His Blood.

Activity

A. Have your older children turn to **Passover Sacrifice (page 56 in the children's activity book)**. Read aloud Exodus 12:3-20. While you read, have children complete the questions. You may wish to have older children look up, read, and complete the worksheet independently.

B. When your children are finished, discuss the answers as a family. Finish your discussion by explaining that it is at this celebration of the Passover meal that Jesus instituted a New and everlasting Covenant and gave us the Eucharist — His Body and Blood.

Answers:

1. Procure for itself a lamb
2. One year old
3. Blemish
4. Slaughter the lambs
5. Blood
6. Hyssop
7. The two doorposts and the lintel
8. Consumed
9. Unleavened bread and bitter herbs
10. Strike down the firstborn
11. Pass over you
12. A day of remembrance

BONUS DISCUSSION
Which religion did Jesus practice?

Age Level: All ages
Recommended time: 5 minutes

Your children, especially younger ones, may be confused about why Jesus would participate in a Jewish festival. In that case, you may want to ask your children, "What religion did Jesus practice?" Recall that God made a covenant with His Chosen People, the Israelites, also known as the Hebrews, or the Jews. The answer then becomes more clear: Jesus was Jewish. He is fully God and fully man, and His earthly family tree is the line of King David, which stretches back to the Father of Faith, Abraham. Many of Jesus' disciples were Jews. So it makes sense not only that they would celebrate the Jewish festival of Passover, but that Jesus would fulfill it as He did at the Last Supper.

In fact, everything Jesus did was a fulfillment of all of God's promises to His Chosen People, the people of Israel. It was God's plan to reveal Himself to the world through one group of people, the people of Israel, so that, when the time was right (or, "in the fullness of time") His plan of salvation could be made known to the world. The plan of salvation was completed in Jesus Christ. Therefore, in the Church Jesus founded, God's chosen people become everyone who accepts Him in faith and love. We are the new Israel.

 ## Connection to the Catechism

By celebrating the Last Supper with his apostles in the course of the Passover meal, Jesus gave the Jewish Passover its definitive meaning. Jesus' passing over to his father by his death and Resurrection, the new Passover, is anticipated in the Supper and celebrated in the Eucharist, which fulfills the Jewish Passover and anticipates the final Passover of the Church in the glory of the kingdom. (CCC 1340)

ACTIVITY 3

Jesus, Our Passover Lamb
SCRIPTURE REFLECTIONS AND ACTIVITY BOOK

Age Level: All ages, with one activity for children ages 5-11 and another for children ages 11 and up

Recommended time: 20 minutes

What you need: Bible, Jesus, Our Passover Lamb Reflections (**page 57** in the children's activity book), Jesus, Our Passover Lamb Booklet (**page 65** in the children's activity book), markers and/or crayons

Adoration of the Mystic Lamb, by Jan van Eyck.

What you need to know before you begin:

At the end of Jesus' public ministry, "the day of the feast of Unleavened Bread arrived, the day for sacrificing the Passover lamb" (Luke 22:7). Jesus gathered the Apostles in the Upper Room for the Last Supper.

Jesus took a cup of wine, and after giving thanks He said, "Take this and share it among yourselves" (Luke 22:17). "Then he took the bread, said the blessing, broke it, and gave it to them, saying, 'This is my body, which will be given for you; do this in memory of me'" (Luke 22:19). Christ instituted the Eucharist and commanded that we eat His Flesh and drink His Blood, signaling His victory over death through His Resurrection.

After He broke and shared the bread, in a similar way He took the cup of wine and said: "This cup is the new covenant in my blood, which will be shed for you" (Luke 22:20). Jesus instituted the Eucharist at the Last Supper as the new and eternal sacrifice. It initiated His new and everlasting Blood Covenant with God's people.

Thus, Jesus became for us our Passover Lamb. This gift would win for all mankind the promise of eternal salvation. The Old Testament Passover lamb, whose blood saved God's people, is replaced by the Lamb of God, Jesus; whose Blood is our eternal salvation. Jesus said "He who eats my flesh and drinks my blood has eternal life, and I will raise him up at the last day" (John 6:54).

Jesus has become the Passover Lamb for all Christians. Using the Greek word *pascha* for the Hebrew word for Passover, St. Paul writes: "For our paschal lamb, Christ, has been sacrificed" (1 Corinthians 5:7). The Church transformed the Jewish Passover from a commemoration of God's freeing the Israelites from slavery to a celebration of Jesus Christ's death and Resurrection, and the freeing of humanity from the slavery of sin and death. God's promise of redemption is available not just to one people, but to the entire world. In Him there is now one, complete sacrifice memorializing and sustaining our own deliverance from sinful captivity.

Activity for Children Ages 11 and Up

A. Ask your older children turn to **Jesus, Our Passover Lamb Reflections (page 57 in the children's activity book)**. Have them read the information and Scripture verses, and then write a brief reflection in response to each.

> **NOTE** You may wish to complete these activities over the course of several days. Don't feel like you and your children have to work on this all at once!

B. When your children have finished, discuss each reflection and help them see that the two books of the Bible — the Old and New Testaments — are complementary and unified. The Last Supper is the New Testament fulfillment of the Old Testament Passover meal. The fulfillment of the Passover at the Last Supper was the institution of the New Covenant in Christ's Blood.

Activity for Children Ages 5-11

A. Ask your younger children to turn to **Jesus, Our Passover Lamb Booklet (page 65 in the children's activity book).** Have them tear out the pages, fold the sheets in half, and staple down the middle "spine" to create a booklet.

B. Then, spend time with your children reading the Scripture verses aloud as they complete the activities.

> **NOTE** You may wish to complete these activities over the course of several days. Don't feel like you and your children have to work on this all at once!

> **Pages 2-3:** Read aloud 1 Corinthians 11:23-26:
> The Lord Jesus on the night when he was betrayed took bread, and when he had given thanks, he broke it, and said, "This is my body which is for you. Do this in remembrance of me." In the same way, after supper he took the cup, saying, "This cup is the new covenant in my blood; do this whenever you drink it, in remembrance of me." For whenever you eat this bread and drink this cup, you proclaim the Lord's death until he comes.

> **Pages 4-5:** Read aloud the story of Moses sacrificing the animal in Exodus 24:3-8:
> When Moses came to the people and related all the words and ordinances of the LORD, they all answered with one voice, "We will do everything that the LORD has told us."
>
> Moses then wrote down all the words of the LORD and, rising early in the morning, he built at the foot of the mountain an altar and twelve sacred stones for the twelve tribes of Israel. Then, having sent young men of the Israelites to offer burnt offerings and sacrifice young bulls as communion offerings to the LORD, Moses took half of the blood and put it in large bowls; the other half he splashed on the altar.
>
> Taking the book of the covenant, he read it aloud to the people, who answered, "All that the LORD has said, we will hear and do."
>
> Then he took the blood and splashed it on the people, saying, "This is the blood of the covenant which the LORD has made with you according to all these words."
>
> Then read aloud Mark 14:24:
> He said to them, "This is my blood of the covenant, which will be shed for many.

- **Pages 6-7:** First, read aloud the story of God providing manna in Exodus 16:9-15 below. Then read aloud John 6:32-51.

  Then Moses said to Aaron, "Tell the whole Israelite community: Approach the LORD, for he has heard your grumbling."

  But while Aaron was speaking to the whole Israelite community, they turned in the direction of the wilderness, and there the glory of the LORD appeared in the cloud!

  The LORD said to Moses: "I have heard the grumbling of the Israelites. Tell them: In the evening twilight you will eat meat, and in the morning you will have your fill of bread, and then you will know that I, the LORD, am your God."

  In the evening, quail came up and covered the camp. In the morning there was a layer of dew all about the camp, and when the layer of dew evaporated, fine flakes were on the surface of the wilderness, fine flakes like hoarfrost on the ground.

  On seeing it, the Israelites asked one another, "What is this?" for they did not know what it was. But Moses told them, "It is the bread which the LORD has given you to eat."

- **Page 9:** Read aloud the story of Jesus feeding the crowd in Matthew 14:15-21:

  When it was evening, the disciples approached him and said, "This is a deserted place and it is already late; dismiss the crowds so that they can go to the villages and buy food for themselves."

  [Jesus] said to them, "There is no need for them to go away; give them some food yourselves."

  But they said to him, "Five loaves and two fish are all we have here."

  Then he said, "Bring them here to me," and he ordered the crowds to sit down on the grass. Taking the five loaves and the two fish, and looking up to heaven, he said the blessing, broke the loaves, and gave them to the disciples, who in turn gave them to the crowds.

  They all ate and were satisfied, and they picked up the fragments left over – twelve wicker baskets full.

- **Page 10:** Read aloud the story of the washing of the disciples' feet in John 13:1-15.

Miracle of the Bread and Fish, by Giovanni Lanfranco.

> **Page 16:** Read aloud the story of the early Christian community in Acts 2:42-47:

They devoted themselves to the teaching of the apostles and to the communal life, to the breaking of the bread and to the prayers.

Awe came upon everyone, and many wonders and signs were done through the apostles.

All who believed were together and had all things in common; they would sell their property and possessions and divide them among all according to each one's need.

Every day they devoted themselves to meeting together in the temple area and to breaking bread in their homes. They ate their meals with exultation and sincerity of heart, praising God and enjoying favor with all the people. And every day the Lord added to their number those who were being saved.

C. For additional guidance on the discussion points, you may refer to the readings on **Jesus, Our Passover Lamb Reflections**.

ACTIVITY 4

Old Covenant, New Covenant
MATCHING ACTIVITY

Age Level: All ages

Recommended time: 5 minutes

What you need: Old Covenant, New Covenant (**page 73** in the children's activity book)

Activity

A. Recall with your children that on the night of the Last Supper, Jesus and His disciples were celebrating the Passover. That night, Jesus instituted the Eucharist as the new and eternal sacrifice – offering the sacrifice of his Body and Blood and becoming our Passover Lamb. The Old Testament Passover lamb, whose blood saved God's people, is replaced by the Lamb of God, Jesus, whose Blood is our eternal salvation.

B. Ask your children turn to **Old Covenant, New Covenant (page 73 in the children's activity book)**. Have them match the characteristics of the Old Covenant to that of the New Covenant established by Christ at the Last Supper.

Answers:

> Blood of a lamb / Blood of Christ

> Freedom from physical slavery / Freedom from slavery to sin

> Celebrate the Passover meal / Celebrate the Last Supper

> An offer to the Chosen People / An offer to all of humanity

> Journey to the Promised Land / Journey to Heaven

> Jews consume the Passover Lamb / Catholics consume the Body and Blood of Christ

LESSON 7

HOLY MASS AND THE EFFECTS OF THE EUCHARIST

Activities and Key Concepts

Activities you will do with your children	Key concepts the activity will teach	Recommended age and time
'This Is My Body' Reading and discussion	At every Mass, bread and wine become the Body and Blood of Jesus Christ.	**Ages:** All ages **Time:** 5–10 minutes
Receiving the Blessed Sacrament Worthily Family discussion	Catholics in a state of grace can and should receive the Eucharist.	**Ages:** All ages **Time:** 5 minutes
The Effects of Holy Communion Grace Person activity	When we receive the Eucharist we are united with Christ, separated from sin, and united with other Christians.	**Ages:** All ages **Time:** 10 minutes

LESSON 7
WORDS TO KNOW

The Words to Know are words that you and your children should know and understand at the end of this month. Use your best judgment about which words to expect each of your children to learn. For older children, you may want to have them create flashcards to help them remember what they have learned.

Altar	The table where a priest offers the sacrifice of the Mass.
Tabernacle	The sacred box where the Eucharist is reserved, or housed. The word tabernacle means "dwelling place."
Transubstantiation	The change that occurs during the Consecration, when bread and wine become the Body and Blood of our Lord, Jesus Christ.

ACTIVITY 1

'This Is My Body'
READING AND DISCUSSION

Age Level: All ages

Recommended time: 5-10 minutes

What you need: 'This Is My Body' (**page 75** in the children's activity book)

Activity

A. Read the essay "This Is My Body" on transubstantiation and have a discussion about it with your children. For younger children, go over the main points at a level that they will understand. Make sure to discuss the following:

  › When the priest says the words of consecration at Mass, the bread and wine are transformed into Jesus' Body and Blood.

  › They do not become symbols of Christ's Body and Blood. They truly become His Body and Blood.

  › The bread and wine have substantially changed (what they are has changed), even though they look the same (their appearance does not change).

B. For older children, have them turn to **'This Is My Body' (page 75 in the children's activity book)** and read the essay, then discuss with them what they read, using these questions to guide your discussion:

  › What are the words the priest says at Mass at the Consecration called?

  › What happens to the bread and the wine when the priest speaks these words?

  › What are the two root words of transubstantiation?

  › What does the word transubstantiation mean?

  › How does the word transubstantiation help you explain the Eucharist?

  › Why is the Eucharist not just a symbol or an idea?

'This Is My Body' Essay

At Mass, when the priest says the words of consecration, "This is my body which will be given up for you ... this is the cup of my blood...," the bread and wine literally become the Body and Blood of our Lord, Jesus Christ. This is a difficult teaching to understand. The Eucharist still looks like bread and wine and when we receive it, it still tastes like bread and wine. But it is truly no longer bread and wine. It has become Jesus' Body and Blood, Soul and Divinity. How does this happen?

We can think about what is necessary for something to be what it is and not something else. For example, what makes a chair a chair rather than a table? A chair has certain necessary characteristics that make it a chair. It does not possess the characteristics to be a table. These necessary characteristics are called "substantial forms." The substantial form of a chair is its "chair-ness." In other words, the substantial form of a chair is what is necessary for a chair to be a chair and not a table, or a banana, or something else entirely. Normally, you cannot change the substantial form of something without changing that thing into something else completely. If you change the substantial form of a chair, it would no longer be a chair. You could take it apart and use the wood and nails to make something else. Then it would become a table, or a stool, or something else entirely.

We can also think about characteristics of something that do NOT make it what

The Savior, by Juan de Juanes.

of does not make it a chair. A chair can be made of wood, or metal, or plastic, or many other types of material. A chair is also not a chair because of its color. A chair could be colored red, or blue, or green. What a chair is made of or what color it is doesn't make a chair what it is. These sorts of characteristics are called "accidents." The word "accident" simply means that even though the characteristic is a part of something, it does not make that something what it is. Color, for example, only makes a chair red, or blue, or green. It does not make a chair a chair, or something else instead. You can even change the accidents of a thing, and it will still be that thing. You can paint a red chair blue, or replace a wooden chair's legs with plastic, and it still remains a chair.

What does any of this have to do with the Eucharist? On one hand, it is enough just to know that by the power of the Holy Spirit, Jesus' Body and Blood, Soul and Divinity become truly present under the appearances of bread and wine. On the other hand, we can describe what happens at Mass during the consecration using the ideas we just learned: substantial forms and accidents.

At Mass, the change of bread and wine into the Real Presence of Jesus is called "transubstantiation." If you look closely at the word transubstantiation, it is made of two parts: the prefix *trans*, which means change, and the root word *substance*. In other words, transubstantiation is a "change of substance."

In the Eucharist, the substantial forms of the bread and wine are transformed into the substantial form of Christ's Body and Blood, Soul and Divinity. That means, the essential characteristics of bread and wine are changed into the essential characteristics of the Body and Blood of Jesus. The now consecrated hosts, however, keep the accidents of bread and wine. In other words, the look, smell, taste, size, shape, and so forth of bread and wine remain. This is why at Mass the bread still looks and tastes like bread. But, hidden beneath those non-essential characteristics of bread and wine is Jesus' Body and Blood, Soul and Divinity.

The Eucharist is 100% Jesus Christ, in substance. It is not just a symbol or an idea. We truly receive Jesus when we receive the Eucharist, just as He told us that He would give us His Flesh to eat and His Blood to drink as true food for the nourishment of our souls.

 ## Connection to the Catechism

It is not man that causes the things offered to become the Body and Blood of Christ, but he who was crucified for us, Christ himself. The priest, in the role of Christ, pronounces these words, but their power and grace are God's. This is my body, he says. This word transforms the things offered. (CCC 1375)

BONUS ACTIVITY
Did Jesus Really Mean the Eucharist Is His Body?

Age Level: All ages
Recommended time: 5 minutes

Read aloud John 6:53-66 or have one of your older children look it up and read it aloud. When you are finished reading, have a discussion on the exchange between Jesus and His disciples. You may use the following questions to begin your discussion:

> What did Jesus say we must do in order to have eternal life? *Eat His flesh and drink His blood.*

> The Bible says that many of Jesus' disciples found this teaching difficult. Why might they find it difficult? *They knew He was speaking literally.*

> Jesus knew that this was a difficult teaching that would probably cause some of His disciples to stop following Him. Did Jesus retract His statement about His flesh and blood, or did He stand by it? *Jesus stood by His statement, showing us that He meant the teaching in a literal way. The Eucharist is not just a symbol — it is truly the Body and Blood of Jesus. We take Jesus at His word!*

ACTIVITY 2

Receiving the Blessed Sacrament Worthily
FAMILY DISCUSSION

Age Level: All ages
Recommended time: 5 minutes

What you need to know before you begin:

Catholics in a state of grace can and should receive the Eucharist. Non-Catholics and Catholics who are in a state of mortal sin may not receive Communion. Some question this decision because they believe it excludes people and causes division among Christians. And the fact is that it does exclude people. But the truth is that when we receive Jesus Christ into our souls, our souls should be ready to give Him a good, pure home. Our souls must be in the state of grace to receive Him worthily. If we are in the state of mortal sin and receive the Eucharist, we commit sacrilege, treating a sacred object unworthily, as if we don't care. The Sacrament of Confession restores grace to the soul and purifies the soul for the Eucharist. (We will learn more about this Sacrament later this year.) For non-Catholics and others who do not believe that the Eucharist is the Lord, to take the Eucharist would be a lie. The *Catechism* and canon law provide for very limited circumstances in which, in case of "grave necessity," such as the danger of death, Sacraments may be administered to those who ask, "provided they manifest the Catholic faith and are properly disposed" (CIC 844 § 4).

Discussion

Go over the information the you read before beginning this lesson about receiving the Eucharist worthily. Make sure your children understand the conditions for receiving Communion:

> Be a practicing Catholic in a state of grace.

> Fast for an hour beforehand.

> Receive respectfully.

NOTE Set a goal to go to Confession at least once a month as a family. Even if your children have not yet made their first Confession, be sure to take them with you. If you are not already in the habit of dressing up for Mass, start that tradition now. Wearing your "Sunday best" is an easy and fun way to set the tone that Mass is something very special.

BONUS ACTIVITY
Holy card craft

Age Level: All ages
Recommended time: 5 minutes
What you need: Holy Card Craft (**page 77** in the children's activity book)

If you are not already spending time in thanksgiving prayer after receiving Holy Communion, resolve to start this month. Have your children turn to **Holy Card Craft (page 77 in the children's activity book)**. Have them tear out the page, cut out the card, then read the prayer. Then, on the back of the card, they should add their own artwork focused on the Eucharist. Have them bring their prayer card with them to Mass for silent prayer after Communion.

 ### Connection to the Catechism

Anyone conscious of a grave sin must receive the sacrament of Reconciliation before coming to communion. (CCC 1385)

To prepare for worthy reception of this sacrament, the faithful should observe the fast required in their Church. Bodily demeanor (gestures, clothing) ought to convey the respect, solemnity, and joy of this moment when Christ becomes our guest. (CCC 1387)

ACTIVITY 3

The Effects of Holy Communion
GRACE PERSON ACTIVITY

Age Level: All ages
Recommended time: 10 minutes
What you need: Grace Person, markers and/or crayons

The Communion of St. Theresa, by Juan Martín Cabezalero.

What you need to know before you begin:

The effects of the Eucharist are three-fold:

> When we receive Holy Communion, we are **united with Jesus Christ**. Our souls are strengthened: we need the Eucharist in the same way our bodies need food. The Eucharist helps us avoid sin and strengthens our charity.

> The Eucharist **separates us from sin**: it forgives venial sin and helps us avoid mortal sin in the future. The Eucharist also helps us see the face of Jesus in the poor. The *Catechism* explains, "Participation in the Holy Sacrifice identifies us

with Jesus' Heart, sustains our strength along the pilgrimage of this life, makes us long for eternal life, and unites us even now to the Church in heaven, the Blessed Virgin Mary, and all the saints" (CCC 1419).

› Receiving the Eucharist **unites us with other Christians**. The very Body of Christ, the Eucharist, strengthens and nourishes the Body of Christ — the Church — whose members are gathered in that Eucharistic celebration: the living on earth (the Church Militant), as well as the saints in Heaven (the Church Triumphant) and the souls in Purgatory (the Church Suffering).

Activity

A. Go over the effects of Holy Communion with your children, explaining them at a level they will understand.

B. Then have your children think of a way to decorate and/or mark your Grace Person to signify each of the effects of Holy Communion. For example, to show that the Eucharist separates us from sin, they might draw and color a halo, and then paste it on the Grace Person's head. Have fun and be creative while learning the effects of the Holy Eucharist.

BONUS ACTIVITY
Eucharist SketchPad video

Age Level: All ages
Recommended time: 6 minutes
What you need: Sophia SketchPad Eucharist video, found at **SophiaSketchPad.org**

Together, watch the six-minute Sophia SketchPad video on the Eucharist. The free video is available at **SophiaSketchPad.org**. When you are finished watching, ask your children what most stood out to them about the video.

St. Thomas Aquinas
SAINT OF THE MONTH

Age Level: All ages
Recommended time: 10 minutes
What you need: St. Thomas Aquinas (**page 79** in the children's activity book), markers and/or crayons

Activity

Read aloud the story of this month's saint to your children. You may also want to show them the full page saint image. While you are reading or sometime the next day, have them complete the coloring page on **page 80** in the children's activity book.

Biography of St. Thomas Aquinas

ST. THOMAS AQUINAS was born in Italy around the year 1224. His father was a count and he had three older brothers and several sisters. When he was nineteen years old he joined the Dominicans, but his family did not want him to be a Dominican monk. So when Thomas was on the road, his brothers came with a troop of soldiers and kidnapped him. They kept him imprisoned in a castle for two years, but during that time Thomas studied theology and memorized large sections of the bible, and his family eventually let him go.

Then Thomas studied at the University of Paris. He was very smart, but he never showed off. The other students gave him the nickname the "Dumb Ox," because he was big and always quiet and humble. One of his classmates, thinking that Thomas was too slow to understand, offered to explain the day's lesson to him. Thomas gratefully accepted his help, but then his classmate became confused over a particularly difficult part in the lesson. So Thomas had to explain the lesson to his classmate because he had understood it all along!

Thomas wrote many books, the most famous being the *Summa theologia*, which explains a large part of the Catholic faith. Thomas also loved Jesus in the Eucharist very much. He wrote about the Eucharist with great prayer, and after he was finished, Jesus appeared to him in a vision and told him, "You have written well of the sacrament of my Body." During his vision, Thomas' body levitated, floating off of the ground. Thomas also wrote many beautiful Eucharistic hymns. We sing two hymns that he wrote, "O salutaris" and "Tantum Ergo," during Benediction.

Near the end of his life, Thomas Aquinas had many mystical visions. These visions filled him with awe and wonder about the mystery of God. He stopped writing because he knew that nothing he wrote could ever compare to God.

Thomas became ill, and when the pope called him to visit a Council, a meeting of the Church, Thomas collapsed on the road and soon after died at about 50 years of age.

Thomas Aquinas is a great example of humility. His feast day is on January 28, and he is the patron saint of Catholic schools, colleges, and universities.

January in Review

THIS MONTH YOU EXPLORED AS A FAMILY THE QUESTIONS:

What is the Eucharist?

Why does Jesus tell us to consume His Body and Blood?

Why and how should we receive Holy Communion?

In Lesson 6 your children learned:

- At every Mass, bread and wine become the Body and Blood of Jesus Christ.
- When we receive the Eucharist we are separated from sin, and united with Christ and other Christians.

In Lesson 7 your children learned:

- All of our Faith flows from, and points toward, Jesus in the Eucharist.
- Jesus instituted the Eucharist at the Last Supper, the fulfillment of the Jewish Passover.

In this space below, write some reflections about the past month. What was your favorite activity? What didn't go as well? Will you adjust anything about what you're doing? What special intentions do you have for next month?

MY NOTES

February

OVERVIEW

VERSE OF THE MONTH

1 JOHN 4:8

Receive the holy Spirit. Whose sins you forgive are forgiven them, and whose sins you retain are retained.

SAINT OF THE MONTH

ST. MARY MAGDALENE

LESSON 8

THE SACRAMENTS OF HEALING

Overview

The aim of this lesson is for your children to understand that Jesus Christ came to bring healing to both our bodies and our souls. It was His desire that, through the ministry of his Church, spiritual and physical healing would continue to be available for all of time.

Catechism Articles to Read

> 1421

> 1426-1428

> 1443

> 1503-1505

Words to Know

> Conversion

LESSON 9
PENANCE AND RECONCILIATION

Overview

In this lesson your children explore the Sacrament of Penance and Reconciliation. In this Sacrament, our sins are forgiven and we are reconciled to God and His Church through the confession of those sins and acts of penance. We are also strengthened by this Sacrament to avoid sin in the future.

Catechism Articles to Read

- 1445
- 1448-1449
- 1451
- 1453
- 1457
- 1459
- 1467
- 1495
- 1498

Words to Know

- Sacrament of Penance and Reconciliation
- Absolution

BY THE END OF THIS MONTH, YOUR CHILDREN SHOULD BE ABLE TO:

- ✔ Recite this month's Scripture Memorization

- ✔ Define this month's Words to Know

- ✔ Identify in Scripture examples of Christ healing illness and suffering and forgiving sins

- ✔ Know how to receive the Sacrament of Penance and Reconciliation

- ✔ Tell you about St. Mary Magdalene

YOUR
Catholic Home
FEAST OF CANDLEMAS

Forty days after the birth of Jesus, the Blessed Virgin Mary went to the Temple in Jerusalem for purification and to offer a sacrifice according to Jewish law. There she met Simeon and Anna, who recognized the promised Messiah. Simeon prophesied that Mary's heart would be pierced by a sword. Catholics celebrate the feast of the Presentation of Christ in the Temple, otherwise known as the Purification of the Blessed Virgin, or Candlemas, 40 days after Christmas on February 2. The Gospel of John calls Jesus the light that shines in the darkness, and the rite of the blessing of the candles recalls the word of Simeon, declaring that Jesus is "the Light for revelation to the Gentiles."

Practice It!

Celebrate this feast by going to Mass and bringing candles for your priest to bless. When you return home, light your candles and hold a Candlemas procession in your home, singing the "Salve Regina" or another Marian hymn. Close by praying the Joyful Mysteries of the Rosary. Then place your candles in your home prayer space to be used for the rest of the year.

Celebrate!

ST. MARY MAGDALENE
JULY 22

I have seen the Lord.
—St. Mary Magdalene
(St. Mary Magdalene is the patron saint of re-
pentant sinners. Her feast day is July 22.)

THINGS TO DO THIS MONTH:

1 Receive the Sacrament of Reconciliation and resolve to go to Confession regularly.

2 Pray together for our pope on the feast day of the Chair of St. Peter, February 22.

VERSE OF THE MONTH
JOHN 20:22-23

Receive the holy Spirit. Whose sins you forgive are forgiven them, and whose sins you retain are retained.

REMEMBER!

The Sacrament of God's forgiveness includes two essential elements: Actions of the Penitent and The Action of God.

MEMORIZE! The Sacrament of Penance and Reconciliation is God's provision for the forgiveness of sins committed after Baptism.

ST. MARY MAGDALENE

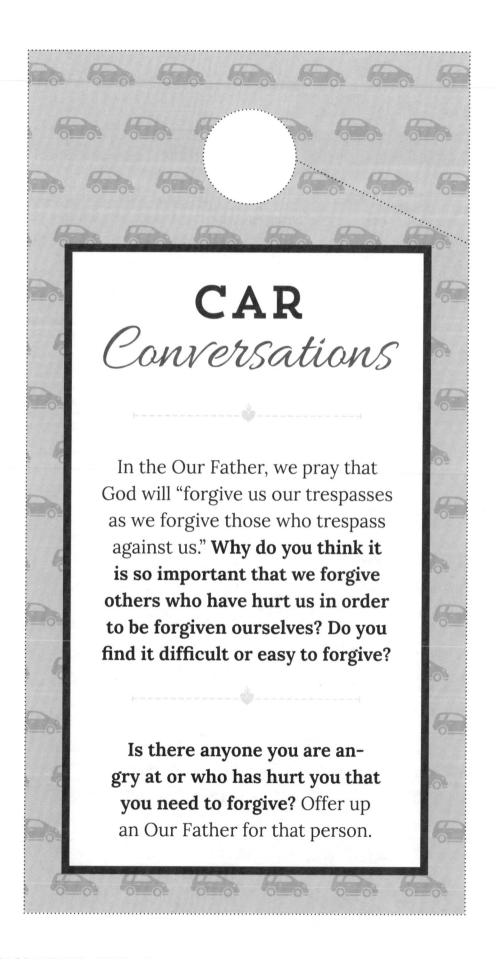

CAR
Conversations

In the Our Father, we pray that God will "forgive us our trespasses as we forgive those who trespass against us." **Why do you think it is so important that we forgive others who have hurt us in order to be forgiven ourselves? Do you find it difficult or easy to forgive?**

Is there anyone you are angry at or who has hurt you that you need to forgive? Offer up an Our Father for that person.

LESSON 8

THE SACRAMENTS OF HEALING

Activities and Key Concepts

Activities you will do with your children	Key concepts the activity will teach	Recommended age and time
God Comforts Us in the Sacraments of Healing Family discussion	Jesus heals both our bodies and souls.	**Ages:** All ages **Time:** 10 minutes
Healing Spiritual and Physical Sickness Discussion and worksheet	Confession heals us from spiritual sickness and death. In the Anointing of the Sick we can receive physical healing and strength for our final journey to God.	**Ages:** Ages 8 and up **Time:** 10 minutes

LESSON 8

WORDS TO KNOW

The Words to Know are words that you and your children should know and understand at the end of this month. Use your best judgment about which words to expect each of your children to learn. For older children, you may want to have them create flashcards to help them remember what they have learned.

Conversion	A heartfelt sorrow for our sins, brought about by the love and grace of God, and a turning toward God with our whole life.

Please choose from the activities for the month.

It is not necessary to complete every activity. We offer a wealth of activities to choose from because each child learns differently, so select the activities that best suit the learning needs of you family. Feel free to shorten or improvise on each activity as necessary. You know best what your family needs!

ACTIVITY 1

God Comforts Us in the Sacraments of Healing

FAMILY DISCUSSION

Age Level: All ages
Recommended time: 10 minutes

What you need to know before you begin:

Jesus gave the Church seven Sacraments – Baptism, Confirmation, Eucharist, Penance and Reconciliation, Anointing of the Sick, Holy Orders, and Holy Matrimony. The Catholic Church identifies two of these, the Sacraments of Penance and Reconciliation and of the Anointing of the Sick, as the Sacraments of Healing (CCC 1421). These Sacraments address both forms of sickness and death that all people experience – physical and spiritual. Though we all experience them, neither was a part of God's original plan for us.

The very first passage of the *Catechism* teaches that "God, infinitely perfect and blessed in himself, in a plan of sheer goodness freely created man to make him share in his own blessed life" (CCC 1). God created us for incorruption – meaning that we were not meant to experience sickness or decay. And He made us in the image of His own eternity – meaning that were meant to live forever. God did not make death and does not delight in the death of the living. Death and sickness entered the world only through the devil's envy and man's sin (Wisdom 1:13; 2:23-24; 1 Corinthians 15:21; Romans 5:12). "As a result, the whole life of men, both individual and social, shows itself to be a struggle, and a dramatic one, between good and evil, between light and darkness" (CCC 1707).

But Scripture also tells us that Jesus came into the world to destroy the works of the devil (1 John 3:8), to restore us to a full and abundant life (John 10:10), and to set us free from the bondage of sin (Romans 8:21; John 8:34-36). Thus, Jesus Christ, the Divine Physician, came to bring healing to both our bodies and our souls. When He walked this earth, Jesus showed tremendous compassion to those who were sick. "His compassion toward all who suffer goes so far that he identifies himself with them: 'I was sick and you visited me'" (CCC 1503). Jesus gave the two Sacraments of Healing—the Sacraments of Penance and Reconciliation and of the Anointing of the Sick—so that the Church could continue the work of restoration and healing until He comes again.

Discussion

A. Ask your children to think of and list people or things that bring them comfort.

B. Next, ask your children to tell you about times when they needed comforting, and encourage them to describe how they felt. Did they need comfort because they were in physical pain (e.g., they were sick with the flu) or were they in emotional pain (e.g., they had just fought with a friend or lost a pet or a loved one)?

C. Help your children understand that everyone experiences pain and heartache, grief and suffering. Everyone experiences these things in different ways and at different times in their lives.

D. Explain to your children that God feels our pain and sorrow and heals us in the Sacraments of Penance and Reconciliation and of the Anointing of the Sick, the Sacraments of Healing. When Jesus walked this earth, He had tremendous compassion for sinners and those who were sick and performed many miracles of healing peoples' bodies and souls.

 Connection to the Catechism

The Lord Jesus Christ, physician of our souls and bodies, who forgave the sins of the paralytic and restored him to bodily health, has willed that his Church continue, in the power of the Holy Spirit, his work of healing and salvation, even among her own members. (CCC 1421)

ACTIVITY 2

Healing Spiritual and Physical Sickness
DISCUSSION AND WORKSHEET

Age Level: Ages 8 and up

Recommended time: 10 minutes at the kitchen table

What you need: Sacraments of Healing (**page 84** in the children's activity book)

Christ and the Samaritan Woman at the Well, by Annibale Carracci.

What you need to know before you begin:

After Baptism, it is the Sacrament of Penance and Reconciliation that heals us from both spiritual sickness (by the forgiveness of venial sins) and spiritual death (by the forgiveness of mortal sins). Through it, our relationship with God is restored. Only God can forgive sins, and those to whom He has entrusted the power to do so, in His name. Thankfully, He has made this power readily available to us through His priests (CCC 986-987).

In the Anointing of the Sick we can receive healing for our physical illnesses (if that is what is best for our soul) and strength for our final journey to God. In addition to the anointing we can receive the Eucharist as Viaticum – "food for the journey." This can be a great spiritual help to us because, "as bodily nourishment restores lost strength, so the Eucharist strengthens our charity, which tends to be weakened in daily life" (CCC 1394). "The reception of the Body and Blood of Christ, at the time of one's "passing over" to God the Father, is a great source of encouragement as we recall Jesus' words in the Gospel of John: "He who eats my flesh and drinks my blood has eternal life, and I will raise him up on the last day" (John 6:54).

Activity

A. Explain to your children that Jesus is the Divine Physician and that He takes care of both our physical and spiritual needs, healing our bodies and our souls.

B. Have your children write the Lord's Prayer in the space provided on the **Sacraments of Healing (page 84 in the children's activity book).**

C. Then, have them rewrite each petition of the Lord's Prayer in the correct column, identifying it as referring to a physical need or a spiritual need.

   Answers: All petitions are spiritual needs, but "Thy will be done, on earth..." and "Give us this day, our daily bread" have both spiritual and physical components.

D. Help your children think of a symbol for the Sacraments of Healing that represents God's glory made known through these Sacraments.

 ### Connection to the Catechism

The Lord Jesus Christ, physician of our souls and bodies, who forgave the sins of the paralytic and restored him to bodily health, has willed that his Church continue, in the power of the Holy Spirit, his work of healing and salvation, even among her own members. This is the purpose of the two sacraments of healing: the sacrament of Penance and the sacrament of Anointing of the Sick. (CCC 1421)

LESSON 9

PENANCE AND RECONCILIATION

Activities and Key Concepts

Activities you will do with your children	Key concepts the activity will teach	Recommended age and time
What Is the Sacrament of Penance and Reconciliation? Family discussion	Confession was instituted by Jesus as a gift of God's mercy.	**Ages:** All ages **Time:** 10 minutes
God's Love and Compassion Scripture reading and sacred art reflection	God always forgives us when we come to him with a contrite heart and ask His forgiveness.	**Ages:** All ages **Time:** 15 minutes
The Power to Forgive Family Scripture reading	Jesus granted His Apostles the authority to hear and forgive sins.	**Ages:** All ages **Time:** 10 minutes
Jesus Welcomes Sinners Who Ask Forgiveness Family Scripture reflection	Jesus brought forgiven sinners back into the community of the People of God.	**Ages:** Ages 8 and up **Time:** 15 minutes
Two Kinds of Sin Family *Catechism* study	Confession of mortal sins is necessary to restore grace to our souls.	**Ages:** All ages **Time:** 15 minutes

LESSON 9

PENANCE AND RECONCILIATION

Activities and Key Concepts
(continued)

Activities you will do with your children	Key concepts the activity will teach	Recommended age and time
The Sacrament of God's Forgiveness Creative activity	Confession includes the actions of the penitent and the actions of God.	**Ages:** All ages **Time:** 10 minutes
Steps to a Good Confession Examination of consceince and family role-play	Confession restores us to the dignity and blessings of the life of the children of God.	**Ages:** All ages **Time:** 20 minutes
The Keys of St. Peter Grace Person activity	Crossed keys are a symbol of the Sacrament of Penance and Reconciliation.	**Ages:** All ages **Time:** 5 minutes

LESSON 9

WORDS TO KNOW

The Words to Know are words that you and your children should know and understand at the end of this month. Use your best judgment about which words to expect each of your children to learn. For older children, you may want to have them create flashcards to help them remember what they have learned.

Sacrament of Penance and Reconciliation	The way in which we receive God's forgiveness for our sins committed after Baptism.
Absolution	An essential element of the Sacrament of Penance and Reconciliation in which the priest, by the power entrusted to the Church of Christ, pardons the sins of the penitent

ACTIVITY 1

What Is the Sacrament of Penance and Reconciliation?
FAMILY DISCUSSION

Age Level: All ages

Recommended time: 10 minutes in your home prayer space

The Confession. by Giuseppe Molteni.

What you need to know before you begin:

In the Sacrament of Penance and Reconciliation, God enables us to satisfy our longings for reconciliation, which is why the *Catechism* calls it a Sacrament of Healing (CCC 1421). After Baptism it is this Sacrament that provides spiritual healing through the forgiveness of sins and the restoration of our relationship with God.

This Sacrament was instituted by Jesus as a gift of God's mercy. In the Sacrament of Penance and Reconciliation, we confess our sins to God (through the priest), and the priest assigns us a penance – usually prayers to say or a good deed to perform. To make a good confession, we must have contrition (or sorrow) for our sins, sincerely commit to work at not sinning again, and, as much as possible, avoid the circumstances that tempt us to sin. In turn, God, through His minister the priest, absolves us of our sins.

The Sacrament of Penance and Reconciliation is sometimes called the Sacrament of Joy because of the tremendous benefits it gives us. God's love is imparted to the sinner, who is restored to His grace and strengthened to sin no more. The Sacrament brings about a "spiritual resurrection," restoring the dignity and blessings of the life of the children of God. The sinner gains an intimate friendship with God and is reconciled with the Church, repairing and restoring his relationships with others. The Sacrament reconciles the sinner with himself in his inmost being, enabling him to regain his true identity as a dearly loved child of God.

The Sacrament of Penance and Reconciliation makes us spiritually stronger and enables us to avoid repeating the sins that we have confessed. Is it any wonder that the Church strongly recommends the confession of everyday faults (venial sins) and teaches that regular confession helps form our conscience, fights against evil tendencies, heals us through Christ, and enables us to progress in the spiritual life (CCC 1458)?

Activity

A. Tell your children an anecdote from your experiences as a child when you made a wrong choice (committed a sin). Explain how you felt in your heart. Did you hurt someone else by this choice? How did you make things right again?

B. As you tell your story, help your children to understand the concept of sin as it relates to consequences, mercy, and forgiveness.

C. Then stress the three important elements of asking for forgiveness: (1) I'm sorry; (2) Please forgive me; (3) I won't do it again.

D. Share how Jesus gives us, through the Sacrament of Penance and Reconciliation, an amazing opportunity to receive forgiveness for hurting ourselves, others, and God. Jesus is a merciful God who will always forgive our sins when we ask forgiveness in Confession because His love for us is greater than all sin.

E. Together say the following prayer, asking God for forgiveness and peace.

O Lord, Jesus Christ, Redeemer and Savior, forgive us our sins, just as you forgave Peter's denial and those who crucified you. Count not our transgressions, but, rather our tears of repentance. Remember not our iniquities, but, rather, our sorrows for the offenses we have committed against you. We long to be true to your Word, and we pray that you will always dwell within us. We promise to give you praise and glory in love and in service all the days of my life.

Connection to the Catechism

The confession (or disclosure) of sins, even from a simply human point of view, frees us and facilitates our reconciliation with others. Through such an admission man looks squarely at the sins he is guilty of, takes responsibility for them, and thereby opens himself again to God and to the communion of the Church in order to make a new future possible. (CCC 1455)

ACTIVITY 2

God's Love and Compassion
SCRIPTURE READING AND SACRED ART REFLECTION

Age Level: All ages
Recommended time: 15 minutes

What you need to know before you begin:

Our God is a God of deep love and unending mercy. He desires that not one of us be lost or far from Him. Through the Sacrament of Penance and Reconciliation, He continually reaches out to us with His arms of pardon and peace. Nothing we can confess is unforgivable or beyond His mercy.

Activity

A. Show your children the art on the next page while you read aloud or take turns reading aloud with your children the Parable of the Prodigal Son in Luke 15:11-32. Then ask your children the following questions:

1. How do you think the father felt when his son asked to have his inheritance before his father died? This would have been a grave insult at the time. *He must have felt sad, hurt, and worried about his son.*

2. Do you think the son cared about how his father felt or even about the inheritance his father had given him? *No, or he wouldn't have asked for his inheritance and squandered it so easily.*

3. How would you describe the state of the father and son's relationship? *Hurt or broken.*

Return of the Prodigal Son. by Bartolomé Esteban Murillo.

4. How did the son feel after he had squandered (or wasted) his inheritance and was poor and suffering? *Sorry that he had done what he did. He realized that even his father's servants were better off than he was.*

5. How do you think the father felt after the son returned and asked for his forgiveness? *Overjoyed that his son had returned!*

6. How do you think the son felt after his father not only accepted his apology, but then throws him a magnificent banquet? *Grateful and humbled that his father is so loving.*

7. How would you now describe the relationship between the father and the son? *Healed, and maybe even stronger than it was before.*

B. Explain to your children that when Jesus told a parable, it was always an earthly story with a heavenly meaning. Just as the father in the story longed for the return of his son, was filled with joy at his return, and forgave his son, God the Father longs for us, is joyful when we return, and always forgives us — no matter what our offense against Him. We only need to come to Him with a contrite heart (sorry for what we have done) and ask for His forgiveness.

BONUS ACTIVITY
The Prodigal Son in Sacred Art

Age Level: All ages

Recommended time: 5 minutes

What yu need: The Prodigal Son (**page 85** in the children's activity book)

Take time to look at the painting of the *Return of the Prodigal Son* by Rembrandt. Then as a family, reflect on how this story shows the love and compassion of God. You may wish to discuss questions like:

> - How would you describe this painting?
> - Can you identify the father and the son?
> - What does the posture of the son tell you?
> - What does the posture of the father tell you?
> - Can you find three differences and three similarities between this painting and the one from the last activity (*Return of the Prodigal Son*, by Bartolomé Esteban Murillo)?

Connection to the Catechism

When he celebrates the sacrament of Penance, the priest is fulfilling the ministry of the Good Shepherd who seeks the lost sheep, of the Good Samaritan who binds up wounds, of the Father who awaits the prodigal son and welcomes him on his return, and of the just and impartial judge whose judgment is both just and merciful. The priest is the sign and the instrument of God's merciful love for the sinner. (CCC 1465)

ACTIVITY 3

The Power to Forgive
FAMILY SCRIPTURE READING

Age level: All ages

Recommended time: 10 minutes, around the kitchen table

What you need: Bible

Christ Giving the Keys of the Kingdom to St. Peter, by Pietro Perugino.

What you need to know before you begin:

Jesus granted His Apostles the authority to hear and forgive sins when he said, "Whose sins you forgive are forgiven them, and whose sins you retain are retained" (John 20:23). Such a verbal confession is in keeping with the requirements of our human nature, as the *Catechism* explains: "Confession to a priest is an essential part of the sacrament of Penance...'for if the sick person is too ashamed to show his wound to the doctor, the medicine cannot heal what it does not know'" (CCC 1456).

Activity

A. Read John 20:19-23 together. (Encourage your children to find the chapter and verses in the Bible by themselves.)

> On the evening of that first day of the week, when the doors were locked, where the disciples were, for fear of the Jews, Jesus came and stood in their midst and said to them, "Peace be with you."
>
> When he had said this, he showed them his hands and his side. The disciples rejoiced when they saw the Lord. [Jesus] said to them again, "Peace be with you. As the Father has sent me, so I send you."
>
> And when he had said this, he breathed on them and said to them, "Receive the holy Spirit. Whose sins you forgive are forgiven them, and whose sins you retain are retained."

B. Explain how in the Gospel of John, Jesus gives the Apostles a gift: the Holy Spirit. Ask your children the following questions, and use the talking point to generate a discussion.

1. How did Jesus pass on the gift of the Holy Spirit to the Apostles? *He breathed on them. The Holy Spirit gave the Apostles the power to forgive in the name of Jesus, instituting the Sacrament of Penance and Reconciliation.*

2. What does it mean to forgive someone? *Forgiving someone means restoring our relationship with that person after he or she has wronged [or: hurt] us. Explain to your child that many times, when someone has done something to hurt us, that person feels sorry and wants to make things right again.*

3. What happens when we forgive someone? *We and the person we forgive feel peace in our hearts. This week, encourage your children to make a special effort not to hurt anyone, and if someone hurts them, remind them to say, "I forgive you."*

4. What happens when God forgives us? *We restore our relationship with God. We grow closer to God and continue on our journey to Heaven.*

5. Who are the successors to the Apostles, and how do we receive God's forgiveness today? *Catholic bishops and priests, as the successors to the Apostles, are able to offer healing and union with God through the power of the Holy Spirit in the Sacrament of Penance and Reconciliation.*

BONUS ACTIVITY
Your Sins Are Forgiven

Age level: 8 and up
Recommended time: 5 minutes around the kitchen table
What you need: Bible, Your Sins Are Forgiven (**page 86** in the children's activity book)

Help your older children to complete the fill in the blank activity. Then have them reflect on the questions that follow, writing their responses.

Answers:

Remember, Jesus came to bring <u>reconciliation</u> and salvation to all <u>people</u>. No matter how often we <u>sin</u> or wander away from Him, He will always give us the opportunity to be <u>forgiven</u>, to be reconciled, and to come <u>home</u> again. So He said to His <u>Apostles</u>, "Receive the <u>Holy Spirit</u>. If you forgive the sins of any, they are forgiven them; if you retain the sins of any, they are retained." With these words, He gave the first priests, His Apostles, the power to <u>forgive sins</u>. And this same power of forgiving sins He gives to all <u>bishops</u> and <u>priests</u> of the Catholic Church.

ACTIVITY 4

Jesus Welcomes Sinners Who Ask Forgiveness
FAMILY SCRIPTURE REFLECTION

Age level: Ages 8 and up

Recommended time: 15 minutes around the kitchen table

What you need: Bible, Jesus Welcomes Sinners Who Ask Forgiveness (**page 87** in the children's activity book)

Christ and the Sinner. by Henryk Siemiradzki.

What you need to know before you begin:

At the time of Jesus, Jewish laws were strong and clear about sin. Sin meant being unclean as well as being separated from the community. In contrast to this law, Jesus showed concern for sinners and love for those who asked for forgiveness.

Activity

A. Have your older children find and read each Scripture passage and record on **Jesus Welcomes Sinners Who Ask Forgiveness (page 87 in the children's activity book)** how Jesus welcomes the sinner.

1. **Luke 15:1-2:** Jesus welcomes sinners and eats with them.

2. **Mark 2:13-17:** Jesus calls on Levi and eats with sinners. Jesus came to save sinners.

3. **Luke 19:5-10:** Jesus asks to stay at Zacchaeus's home.

4. **Luke 17:3-4:** Forgive every time.

B. Next, ask your children to reflect on the following reference from the *Catechism* no. 1443: "Jesus reintegrated forgiven sinners into the community of the People of God from which sin had alienated or even excluded them." Explain briefly how Jesus is a role model to all of us. Why is it important to welcome sinners back into the community?

 Connection to the Catechism

During his public life Jesus not only forgave sins, but also made plain the effect of this forgiveness: he reintegrated forgiven sinners into the community of the People of God from which sin had alienated or even excluded them. A remarkable sign of this is the fact that Jesus receives sinners at his table, a gesture that expresses in an astonishing way both God's forgiveness and the return to the bosom of the People of God. (CCC 1443)

ACTIVITY 5

Two Kinds of Sin
FAMILY CATECHISM STUDY

Age level: All ages
Recommended time: 15 minutes around the kitchen table
What you need: Two Kinds of Sin (**page 88** in the children's activity book)

What you need to know before you begin:

Just like physical injuries damage or kill our bodies, sins damage our souls. All sins are bad, but some are worse than others. Venial sins hurt our relationship with God. They weaken charity, impede the soul's progress in the exercise of the virtues, and merit temporal punishment. In addition, deliberate and unrepented venial sin disposes us little by little to commit mortal sin. However venial sin does not break the covenant with God. With God's grace it is humanly reparable.

Mortal sins, on the other hand, cut us off from God. Committing a mortal sin is a spiritual death. We cannot receive the Eucharist when we are in a state of mortal sin, just as a dead person is not helped by eating food.

A mortal sin requires three conditions:
› The object (sin committed) is grave matter.
› It is committed with full knowledge.
› It is done with deliberate consent.

A person commits a venial sin in two cases:
› When he does not observe God's law in a less serious matter.
› When he does not have full knowledge or give full consent in a grave matter.

Activity

A. Help your children understand the difference between mortal and venial sin by assisting them to complete the matching activity on **Two Kinds of Sin (page 88 in the children's activity book)**.

B. Emphasize that mortal sin cuts us off from God, and that confessing it is necessary to restore grace in our souls. We may not receive Holy Communion if we have unconfessed mortal sin.

C. Continue to explain that confessing venial sins is important as well, because it helps us form our consciences and avoid future sin.

Answers:

1. Venial
2. Mortal
3. Venial

4. Venial
5. Mortal
6. Venial

7. Mortal
8. Venial
9. Mortal

BONUS ACTIVITY
Making the Right Choice

Age Level: All ages
What you need: Making the Right Choice (**page 89** in the children's activity book)

To help your children understand that sin is a choice, explain that God made us to be His children. And as children of God, we have a body, like animals, and a soul, like angels. We are created differently from animals because we have the ability to love and serve God.

We are all created in the image and likeness of God. This means that God gave us minds to think and make choices. We have been given the freedom to choose between good and bad. God is a loving Father and wants us to be happy. He knows that the only way we can be happy is to choose good and say no to sin. The problem is that sometimes doing the wrong thing looks good.

Have your children respond to the scenarios on **Making the Right Choice (page 89 in the children's activity book)**. Your children may say their answers aloud or write them down.

ACTIVITY 6

The Sacrament of God's Forgiveness
CREATIVE ACTIVITY

Age level: All ages (younger children may color the pictures)
Recommended time: 10 minutes, your children working while you are making dinner
What you need: The Sacrament of God's Forgiveness (**page 90** in the children's activity book), markers and/or crayons

What you need to know before you begin:

The Sacrament of God's Forgiveness or Penance and Reconciliation consists of two "equally essential elements" (CCC 1448). The first element is the action of the penitent, and the second the action of God.

The three actions of the penitent, the one seeking forgiveness:

1. Contrition
2. Confession of Sin
3. Satisfaction

The three actions of God through the minister of His Church (the priest):

1. Absolution of our sins
2. Determination of the necessary penance
3. Prayer for the sinner

Activity

A. Explain to your children that the Sacrament of Penance and Reconciliation, also known as the Sacrament of God's Forgiveness, consists of two "equally essential elements" (CCC 1448). In other words, it must always include two parts. The first element is the action of the penitent, and the second the action of God.

B. As your children color the pictures, read the information aloud to learn more about the Sacrament of God's Forgiveness. We know that through this Sacrament we receive God's grace to help keep our souls free from sin and to help us love Jesus more.

BONUS ACTIVITY
Confession SketchPad video

Age Level: All ages
Recommended time: 6 minutes
What you need: Sophia SketchPad Confession video, found at
SophiaSketchPad.org

Together, watch the six-minute Sophia SketchPad video on Confession. The free video is available at **SophiaSketchPad.org**. When you are finished watching, ask your children what they might say to someone who said he was scared to confess his sins.

 ### Connection to the Catechism

Beneath the changes in discipline and celebration that this sacrament has undergone over the centuries, the same fundamental structure is to be discerned. It comprises two equally essential elements: on the one hand, the acts of the man who undergoes conversion through the action of the Holy Spirit: namely, contrition, confession, and satisfaction; on the other, God's action through the intervention of the Church. The Church, who through the bishop and his priests forgives sins in the name of Jesus Christ and determines the manner of satisfaction, also prays for the sinner and does penance with him. Thus the sinner is healed and re-established in ecclesial communion. (CCC 1448)

ACTIVITY 7

Steps to a Good Confession
FAMILY ROLE-PLAY

Age level: All ages

Recommended time: 20 minutes

What you need: Bible, A Personal Examination of Conscience (**page 92** in the children's activity book), Steps to a Good Confession (**page 94** in the children's activity book)

What you need to know before you begin:

If you did not read the information in **Activity 1: What is the Sacrament of Penance and Reconciliation**, please be sure to go back and read that section before proceeding with this activity.

Activity

A. Read aloud from Luke 19:1-10, the story of Zacchaeus the Tax Collector. Zacchaeus receives forgiveness after he seeks Jesus (he is sorry for his sins), and then he makes things right again (penance) by promising to give half of his possessions to the poor.

B. Then give your children time to reflect on **A Personal Examination of Conscience (page 92 in the children's activity book)**. This experience will help your children understand what areas of their lives may not be in line with God's directions on how we are to live.

Discussion

A. Discuss with your children how they feel when they know they have done something against God. A feeling of guilt is our conscience telling us that we have made a wrong choice and have distanced ourselves from God. Feeling sorry for our choices is the first step for the Sacrament of Penance and Reconciliation.

B. Together, read and discuss the information on **Steps to a Good Confession (page 94 in the children's activity book)**. Discussion points include:

> **Examine your conscience:** Discuss the importance of understanding sin. Your children must know their sins. If they are unsure whether something is a sin, tell them to confess it and ask the priest for guidance.

> **Contrition for your sins:** Tell your children that when they are contrite, they feel sorry about their choices. If they are truly sorry, they will strive to not commit the same sins again.

> **Confess your sins to a priest in Confession:** Encourage your children to be honest and tell all their sins. Remind them that they do not need to be afraid. The priest will not judge them or think badly of them. All priests are bound by the seal of Confession and can never tell anyone what they have heard in Confession.

> **Receive absolution:** You may want to tell your children that absolution is like being washed clean or starting over again on a brand new page. In absolution, you receive God's forgiveness.

> Finally, explain that the last part of Confession is accepting and doing your **penance**. Penance brings your children closer to God by getting them back in the habit of prayer and charity.

C. Remind your children of what you discussed last lesson about the two necessary elements for the Sacrament of Penance and Reconciliation: the actions of the penitent and the actions of God through the priest.

Role-play

Help your children role-play the steps of receiving the Sacrament of Penance and Reconciliation in the proper order. Take turns playing the role of the penitent and the priest. Discuss the following points with your children, and help them understand that they needn't be afraid. God, our Father in Heaven, is merciful and wants us to receive His sacramental grace to keeps us close to Him.

NOTE Emphasize that only the priest needs to hear your sins, and the priest can never reveal to anyone what you have told him – every Confession is an absolute secret! For this role-play you do not need to say your sins aloud.

Zacchaeus in the Sycamore Awaiting the Passage of Jesus by James Tissot.

 Connection to the Catechism

The movement of return to God, called conversion and repentance, entails sorrow for and abhorrence of sins committed, and the firm purpose of sinning no more in the future. Conversion touches the past and the future and is nourished by hope in God's mercy. (CCC 1490)

BONUS ACTIVITY
What Is Absolution?

Age Level: Ages 8 and up
Recommended time: 5 minutes

The *Catechism of the Catholic Church* no. 1449 teaches us that:

> The formula of absolution used in the Latin Church expresses the essential elements of this sacrament: the Father of mercies is the source of all forgiveness. He effects the reconciliation of sinners through the Passover of his Son and the gift of his Spirit, through the prayer and ministry of the Church:
>
> > God, the Father of mercies,
> > Through the death and resurrection of his Son
> > Has reconciled the world to himself
> > And sent the Holy Spirit among us
> > For the forgiveness of sins;
> > Through the ministry of the Church
> > May God give you pardon and peace,
> > And I absolve you from your sins
> > In the name of the Father, and the Son and of the Holy Spirit.

Have your children read and reflect on this prayer to help them understand that it is Christ alone who forgives sins (absolves them) through the ministry of the priest or bishop. The word *absolution* means the washing away of sins. Have your children write brief journal reflection on how it feels, or will feel, to receive absolution in Confession.

ACTIVITY 8

The Keys of Saint Peter
GRACE PERSON ACTIVITY

Age level: All ages

Recommended time: 5 minutes

What you need: Crossed Key Symbol (**page 97** in the children's activity book), markers and/or crayons

Activity

A. Explain to your children that a symbol of the papacy is the crossed keys of St. Peter. This is because Jesus gave the Apostle Simon the keys to the Kingdom when He gave him his new name, Peter, which means "rock." (The next time you go to church, see if you can find a statue or picture of St. Peter holding a key!)

B. Make sure that your children understand that these keys are not literal keys, but instead are a symbol for authority. Keys can lock or unlock: keep people out or let them in.

C. These crossed keys are also a symbol of the Sacrament of Penance and Reconciliation because when Jesus gave Peter the keys, He said, "I will give you the keys to the kingdom of heaven. Whatever you bind on earth shall be bound in heaven; and whatever you loose on earth shall be loosed in heaven" (Matthew 16:19). This binding and loosing refers to the Church's authority to forgive sins through the priest *in persona Christi capitis*, "in the person of Christ the Head." The *Catechism* states, "in imparting to his apostles his own power to forgive sins the Lord also gives the authority to reconcile sinners with the Church" (1444).

D. Have your children turn to **Crossed Key Symbol (page 97 in the children's activity book)** and color the two crossed keys, one gold and one silver. The gold key symbolizes the power of the Kingdom of Heaven, and the silver key symbolizes the spiritual authority of the Church on earth.

E. Cut out the keys and paste them on your Grace Person.

St. Mary Magdalene
SAINT OF THE MONTH

Age level: All ages
Recommended time: 10 minutes
What you will need: St. Mary Magdalene (**page 99** in the children's activity book), markers and/or crayons

What you need to know before you begin:

The Western Catholic Tradition identifies three figures in the Bible as Mary Magdalene: the Mary Magdalene named in the Bible, the unnamed sinner who anoints Jesus' feet with oil, and Mary the sister of Lazarus. What is certain is that St. Mary Magdalene's life is a powerful story about the abundance of God's mercy. She was a sinner, a woman possessed by demons. But after Jesus healed her, she followed Him with great love. She did not abandon Him, but remained faithful to Him during His suffering and death on the Cross. With great devotion, she came to anoint His body in the tomb, and her heart broke when she could not find Him. Jesus bestows on her the honor of acting as His first witness to the Resurrection, choosing her as the messenger to His Apostles.

The Greek Church holds that Mary Magdalene retired with our Lady and the Apostle John to Ephesus and there died. From there her relics were moved to Constantinople (now Istanbul, Turkey) in 886.

All sinners can take heart and trust in Jesus' tenderness and mercy when they read about St. Mary Magdalene's life in the Scriptures.

Activity

Read aloud the story of this month's saint to your children. You may also want to show them the full page saint image. While you are reading or sometime the next day, have them complete the coloring page on **page 99** in the children's activity book.

Biography of St. Mary Magdalene

MARY MAGDALENE lived in Galilee during the time of Jesus' life. She was a great sinner and was even possessed by seven demons! One day Jesus found her and cast the demons out of her. Mary Magdalene was so very grateful to Jesus and loved

Him very much. She followed Him as He preached to sinners and took care of Him along with some other women who followed him.

When Jesus was crucified, Mary Magdalene stayed with Him. She remained faithful even though most of Jesus' friends had abandoned Him. She stood at the foot of the Cross along with Jesus' mother, and John, the beloved disciple.

After His death, Jesus was laid in a tomb. Mary Magdalene and some other women went to the tomb to anoint His body with oil according to Jewish custom. But when they looked into the tomb, Jesus' body was missing. They were amazed and sad because they did not know where Jesus' body was. Two angels dressed in white told them not to be amazed that Jesus was gone because He had risen from the dead!

The women ran to tell the Apostles the news that Jesus' body was gone. The Apostles rushed over to see the empty tomb, but afterward they returned home. Mary stayed behind at the tomb, weeping.

Her heart was breaking because she didn't know where Jesus was. She turned around and saw a man standing in front of her. It was Jesus, but she did not recognize Him. She thought He was the gardener.

He asked her, "Woman, why are you weeping? Who are you looking for?"

"Sir, if you carried him away, tell me where you laid him, and I will take him," she begged Him in reply.

Jesus responded to her request with a single word, "Mary."

At her name she recognized Jesus and with great joy fell to His feet, trying to wrap her arms around Him. But Jesus did not let her touch Him because He had still to see His Father. Instead, He sent her to His Apostles to tell them the Good News of His resurrection. She ran to the Apostles as fast as her feet could carry her to tell them the Good News that she had seen Jesus and that He had risen from the dead.

Mary Magdalene is a great example of God's mercy toward sinners. She is the patron saint of penitent sinners and her feast day is July 22.

February in Review

THIS MONTH YOU EXPLORED AS A FAMILY THE QUESTIONS:

What are the Sacraments of Healing?

What happens when we go to Confession?

Why do we need to confess our sins to a priest?

In Lesson 8 your children learned:

> Jesus comforts us in the Sacraments of healing. He heals us of spiritual sickness in Confession. In the Anointing of the Sick we can receive physical healing and strength for our final journey to God.

In Lesson 9 your children learned:

> God forgives the sins committed after Baptism through the Sacrament of Penance and Reconciliation.

> The Sacrament of God's forgiveness includes two essential elements: actions of the penitent and the action of God.

In this space below, write some reflections about the past month. What was your favorite activity? What didn't go as well? Will you adjust anything about what you're doing? What special intentions do you have for next month?

MY NOTES

March
OVERVIEW

VERSE OF THE MONTH

JAMES 5:14

Is anyone among you sick? He should summon the presbyters of the church, and they should pray over him and anoint [him] with oil in the name of the Lord.

SAINT OF THE MONTH

ST. BERNADETTE SOUBIROUS

LESSON 10

THE SACRAMENT OF ANOINTING OF THE SICK

Overview

The aim of this lesson is for your children to understand that God is merciful. Your children will be able to explain the "special grace" from God that we receive during the Sacrament of the Anointing of the Sick. They will also see the relationship between Jesus' healing and the Church's continuation of this healing through the sacrament.

Catechism Articles to Read

> 1517-1525

> 1527-1532

Words to Know

> Anointing of the Sick

> Oil of the Sick

> Sacramental Grace

> Viaticum

LESSON 11
THE TRIDUUM

Overview

This lesson is meant to help you explore the Paschal Triduum, the three holiest day of the Church year, and is meant to be used alongside your family's participation in the Triduum celebrations.

Catechism Articles to Read

> 1168

Words to Know

None for this lesson

BY THE END OF THIS MONTH, YOUR CHILDREN SHOULD BE ABLE TO:

- ✓ Recite this month's Scripture Memorization
- ✓ Define this month's Words to Know
- ✓ Identify the Rite of the Anointing of the Sick and who can receive the Sacrament
- ✓ Participate in and tell you about the liturgical celebrations of the Triduum
- ✓ Tell you about St. Bernadette

YOUR
Catholic Home
PASSIONTIDE

The two weeks before Easter are known as Passiontide. Passiontide is a time when we can in a special way unite our sufferings with Christ. It is marked by solemnity and penitence as we liturgically celebrate the events that lead to Christ's betrayal, suffering, and death on the Cross. To mark this period of penitence, the Church veils all crosses and statues of our Lord and the saints, except for the crosses and images of the Way of the Cross. The crosses are unveiled before the Good Friday celebration and the rest of the statues and images are unveiled before the Easter Vigil Mass.

Practice It!

Hold a veiling ceremony in your home on the day before Palm Sunday. Read the Palm Sunday Gospel together, pray the Sorrowful Mysteries of the Rosary, or sing Lenten hymns such as "Were You There?" "O Sacred Head, Now Wounded," or "My Song Is Love Unknown." Veil any crucifixes in your house. Before you take your family to the Good Friday celebrations, unveil and kiss each crucifix while once again singing Lenten hymns.

Celebrate!

ST. BERNADETTE
APRIL 16

It is loving the Cross that one finds one's heart, for Divine Love cannot live without suffering.
—*St. Bernadette Soubirous*

THINGS TO DO THIS MONTH:

1 Offer up a family rosary for sick relatives and friends.

2 Write and send cards to those you know who are ill or in the hospital.

VERSE OF THE MONTH
JAMES 5:14

Is anyone among you sick? He should summon the presbyters of the church, and they should pray over him and anoint [him] with oil in the name of the Lord.

REMEMBER!

The Sacrament of Anointing of the Sick unites sick persons with the passion of Jesus Christ and consecrates their suffering for participation in the saving work of Christ.

MEMORIZE! By the sacred anointing of the sick and the prayer of the priests the whole Church commends those who are ill to the suffering and glorified Lord, that he may raise them up and save them. (CCC 1499)

ST. BERNADETTE

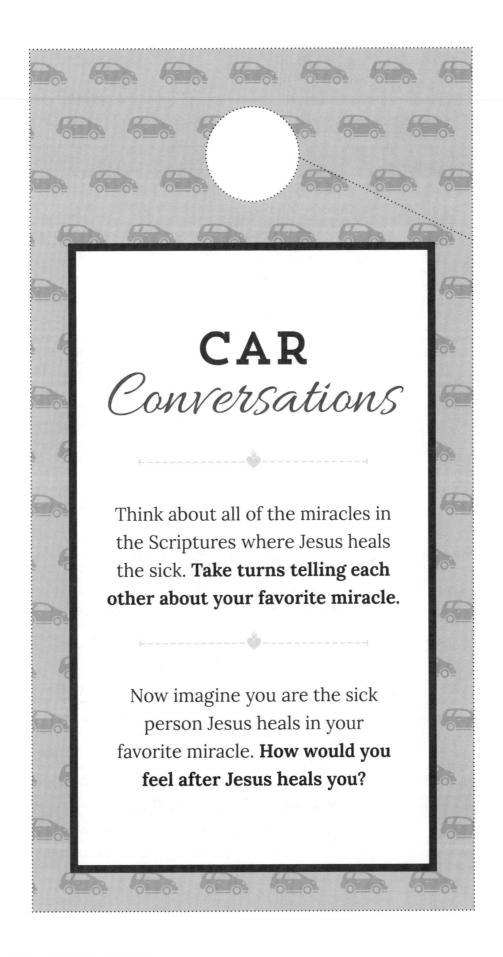

CAR
Conversations

Think about all of the miracles in the Scriptures where Jesus heals the sick. **Take turns telling each other about your favorite miracle.**

Now imagine you are the sick person Jesus heals in your favorite miracle. **How would you feel after Jesus heals you?**

LESSON 10

THE SACRAMENT OF ANOINTING OF THE SICK

Activities and Key Concepts

Activities you will do with your children	Key concepts the activity will teach	Recommended age and time
Jesus' Healing Miracles Scripture reading and activities	Jesus performed many healing miracles as signs that He was the promised Messiah and the Kingdom of God was at hand.	**Ages:** Ages 5-8 **Time:** 10 minutes
Christ Gives Meaning to Our Suffering Family discussion	By His Passion, Jesus transformed the meaning of suffering.	**Ages:** All ages **Time:** 10 minutes
The History of the Sacrament of Anointing of the Sick Scripture reading and discussion	Jesus commanded the Apostles to heal the sick in His name. Bishops and priests have this authority.	**Ages:** All ages **Time:** 15 minutes
Celebrating the Sacrament of Anointing of the Sick Discussion and activity	Priests give this Sacrament to those in danger of death through the laying on of hands, prayer, and anointing of their head and hands.	**Ages:** All ages **Time:** 15 minutes

LESSON 10

THE SACRAMENT OF ANOINTING OF THE SICK

Activities and Key Concepts (continued)

Activities you will do with your children	Key concepts the activity will teach	Recommended age and time
The Effects of Anointing of the Sick Discussion and crossword puzzle	Those who receive it are strengthened against fear, united to Christ, and prepared for the final journey.	**Ages:** Ages 8 and up **Time:** 10 minutes
The Oil of Anointing Grace Person activity	Review of the rite of Anointing of the Sick.	**Ages:** All ages **Time:** 5 minutes

LESSON 10

WORDS TO KNOW

The Words to Know are words that you and your children should know and understand at the end of this month. Use your best judgment about which words to expect each of your children to learn. For older children, you may want to have them create flashcards to help them remember what they have learned.

Anointing of the Sick	The Anointing of the Sick is the Sacrament in which the Church prays for and anoints with sacred oil those who are gravely ill, asking for strength and healing.
Oil of the Sick	The Holy Oil used in the Anointing of the Sick. This oil is a sign of nourishment, healing, and strength.
Sacramental Graces	The supernatural help we receive from God through the Sacraments. In the Anointing of the Sick, God gives us the grace to accept our illness and die a good death.
Viaticum	Eucharist that is given to the dying. A sacrament of "passing over" from this life to eternal life.

Please choose from the activities for the month.

It is not necessary to complete every activity. We offer a wealth of activities to choose from because each child learns differently, so select the activities that best suit the learning needs of you family. Feel free to shorten or improvise on each activity as necessary. You know best what your family needs!

ACTIVITY 1

Jesus' Healing Miracles
SCRIPTURE READING AND ACTIVITIES

Age level: Ages 5–8
Recommended time: 10 minutes
What you need: The Cleansing of the Ten Lepers (**page 104** in the children's activity book), Jesus Heals the Sick (**page 105** in the children's activity book), colored pencils

What you need to know before you begin:

Jesus performed many healing miracles as signs that He was the promised Messiah and that the Kingdom of God was at hand. In Matthew's Gospel, we read that John the Baptist sent his disciples to ask Jesus: "Are you the one who is to come, or should we look for another?" Jesus said to them in reply, "Go and tell John what you hear and see: the blind regain their sight, the lame walk, lepers are cleansed, the deaf hear, the dead are raised, and the poor have the good news proclaimed to them" (Matthew 11:3-5).

Discussion

A. Explain to your children that Jesus had a special love for the needy, the sick, and the poor. When Jesus was 30 years old, He began traveling throughout the land to spread the Good News of God. Along the way, He performed many miracles, bringing healing to many people suffering from illness and sin.

Christ and the Lepers, by Gebhard Fugel.

B. Have your children read the story of the Cleansing of the Ten Lepers, Luke 17:11-19, in their activity books, and then write a prayer of thanks to Jesus.

C. Ask your children the following question: Only one leper returned to thank Jesus. What does this man have that the other nine do not?

BONUS ACTIVITY
Jesus Heals the Sick

Age level: All ages
Recommended time: 10 minutes

Together, brainstorm as many of Jesus' healing miracles as you can. Encourage your children to describe their favorite healing miracle of Jesus and ask them to explain why they like the story.

Next, read Mark 8:22-26 and discuss the following questions to help them better understand the healing graces of Jesus:

1. Who asked Jesus to heal the blind man? *The crowd; the blind man's friends.*
2. Where did Jesus take the man to be healed? *Away from the crowd, outside the village.*
3. How many times did Jesus lay His hands on the blind man's eyes? *Two.*
4. Why do you think Jesus cured him in this way? *Let your children come up with their own answers.*

BONUS ACTIVITY

Jesus' Healing Miracles Diorama

Age level: All ages

Recommended time: 30 minutes

What you will need: A shoe box and desired craft materials

Have your children create a diorama of your favorite healing miracle of Jesus. Using a shoe box and materials like scrap fabric, rocks, construction paper, clay, toy figures, felt, etc., have them think through the story they want to represent and lay out all the people and objects important to tell the story of Jesus healing the sick. When their diorama is complete, have them show-and-tell to the whole family.

 Connection to the Catechism

Christ's compassion toward the sick and his many healings of every kind of infirmity are a resplendent sign that "God has visited his people" and that the Kingdom of God is close at hand. (CCC 1503)

ACTIVITY 2

Christic Gives Meaning to Our Suffering
FAMILY DISCUSSION

Age level: All ages
Recommended time: 10 minutes

Christ Wearing the Crown of Thorns, Supported_by_ Angels, by Annibale Carracci.

What you need to know before you begin:

Jesus came to accomplish an even greater healing than physical healing alone. This greater healing He announced was "a more radical healing: the victory over sin and death through his Passover. ...By his passion and death on the cross Christ has given a new meaning to suffering: it can henceforth configure us to him and unite us with his redemptive Passion" (CCC 1505).

Thus, our suffering now has a greater purpose. It is no longer something to be dreaded or feared because it now has redemptive value if we patiently endure it and join it with the suffering of Christ. That is why St. Paul could say, "Now I rejoice in my sufferings for your sake" (Colossians 1:24).

Discussion

A. Ask your children to remember a time when they hurt themselves badly or were very sick. Let them tell you about their memory. Did this time of suffering keep them from doing things they normally would do? Ask them to explain in what way. How did they feel when they became better?

B. Then ask your children:

  › Did anything good come of their suffering, or was it simply completely unpleasant?

  › How would you feel about suffering if nothing good ever came of it?

  › Would your attitude toward suffering change if you discovered that good could come through suffering?

C. Explain that Jesus' death on the Cross completely transformed the nature of suffering. Now we can offer up our pain, illness, and sorrow with Jesus' to make up for our own and other's sins. If we embrace our crosses or trials, we are imitating our Savior, who died on the Cross for our sins. Suffering can make us holy and bring us closer to Jesus!

 Connection to the Catechism

Moved by so much suffering Christ not only allows himself to be touched by the sick, but he makes their miseries his own: "He took our infirmities and bore our diseases." But he did not heal all the sick. His healings were signs of the coming of the Kingdom of God. They announced a more radical healing: the victory over sin and death through his Passover. On the cross Christ took upon himself the whole weight of evil and took away the "sin of the world," of which illness is only a consequence. By his passion and death on the cross Christ has given a new meaning to suffering: it can henceforth configure us to him and unite us with his redemptive Passion. (CCC 1505)

ACTIVITY 3

The History of the Sacrament of Anointing of the Sick

SCRIPTURE READING AND DISCUSSION

Age level: Ages 8 and up

Recommended time: 15 minutes

What you need: Jesus' Healing Miracles (**page 106** in the children's activity book)

What you need to know before you begin:

Jesus gave his twelve Apostles the authority to drive out evil spirits and to heal the sick. He charged them to make this proclamation: "The kingdom of heaven is at hand. Cure the sick, raise the dead, cleanse lepers, drive out demons. Without cost you have received; without cost you are to give" (Matthew 10:7-8).

The *Catechism of the Catholic Church* describes how the Church continues this healing mission: "The Church has received this charge from the Lord and strives to carry it out by taking care of the sick as well as accompanying them with her prayer of intercession" (CCC 1509).

Anointing of the Sick is one of the seven Sacraments of the Church—all of which were instituted by Jesus. It is intended to strengthen those who suffer from illness (CCC 1511). As St. James put it:

Is anyone among you sick? He should summon the presbyters of the church, and they should pray over him and anoint [him] with oil in the name of the Lord, and the prayer of faith will save the sick person, and the Lord will raise him up. If he has committed any sins, he will be forgiven. (James 5:14-15)

Discussion

Explain to your children that the Sacrament of Anointing of the Sick began with the healing miracles of Jesus that you have been learning about. Jesus healed people physically and spiritually, and He instructed His Apostles to do the same. Mark 6:7-13 tells us that Jesus sent His Apostles out in pairs and told them to heal the sick in His name: "They anointed with oil many who were sick and cured them." Bishops and priests have been given this same authority to heal the sick and the dying in Jesus' name, continuing His ministry on earth.

St. Paul Healing the Cripple at Lystra, by Karel Dujardin.

Activity

A. Have your older children turn to **Jesus' Healing Miracles (page 106 in the children's activity book).** Listed on the worksheet are several Scripture passages that detail Jesus' healing miracles.

B. Read these Scripture verses together, encouraging your older children to find each passage on their own so they become more comfortable with their Bibles. Then have them write a brief description of the miracle and write whether the miracle is a spiritual healing or a physical healing.

Answers:

1. **Matthew 8:5-13:** Physical healing; Jesus healed the Centurion's servant.

2. **John 5:1-9:** Physical healing; Jesus healed the sick man by telling him to pick up his mat and walk.

3. **Mark 2:5-6:** Spiritual healing; Jesus forgave the sins of the paralyzed man.

4. **Luke 17:11-14:** Physical healing; Jesus healed the ten lepers.

5. **John 5:14-15:** Spiritual healing; Jesus told the man he had healed to sin no more.

6. **Mark 1:29-31:** Physical healing; Jesus healed Simon's mother-in-law of her fever.

7. **Luke 17:15-19:** Spiritual healing; Jesus offered salvation to the healed Samaritan leper who thanked Jesus for healing him.

8. **John 11:1-44:** Physical healing; Jesus raised his friend Lazarus from the dead.

 Connection to the Catechism

"Heal the sick!" The Church has received this charge from the Lord and strives to carry it out by taking care of the sick as well as by accompanying them with her prayer of intercession. She believes in the life-giving presence of Christ, the physician of souls and bodies. This presence is particularly active through the sacraments, and in an altogether special way through the Eucharist, the bread that gives eternal life and that St. Paul suggests is connected with bodily health. (CCC 1509)

ACTIVITY 4

Celebrating the Sacrament of Anointing of the Sick
DISCUSSION AND ACTIVITY

Age level: All ages

Recommended time: 15 minutes

What you need: Pictures from your child(ren)'s Baptisms, Signs and Symbols of the Sacrament (**page 108** in the children's activity book)

What you need to know before you begin:

The Sacrament of Anointing of the Sick can be received by any baptized Catholic who is in danger of death from sickness, a serious operation, or old age. It can be received more than once – even for the same illness, if that illness gets worse (canons 998, 1004, 1002-1007). The person receiving it does not have to be conscious at the time of reception.

The Anointing can take place in the person's home, in a hospital, or in a church. It can be celebrated for an individual or a group (CCC 1517). It is best celebrated when it includes the Eucharist and after the reception of the Sacrament of Penance and Reconciliation. The celebration is based on the elements found in the letter of St. James: "The 'priests of the Church' – in silence – lay hands on the sick; they pray over them in the faith of the Church. ...They then anoint them with oil blessed, if possible, by the bishop" (CCC 1519).

Only a priest can give the Anointing, with the oil of the sick blessed by the bishop, to a sick person. This Sacrament begins when the priest silently lays his hands on the head of the sick person. In the laying on of hands, the Holy Spirit brings strength and comfort to the person who is suffering. Next, the priest anoints the person's forehead and says, "Through this holy anointing may the Lord in His love and mercy help you with the grace of the Holy Spirit." Finally, the priest anoints the palms of the hands with the "oil of the sick" while praying these words: "May the Lord who freed you from sin save you and raise you up."

The Church also offers the dying person the Eucharist as Viaticum – "food for the journey." This is in response to Jesus' promise that "whoever eats my flesh and drinks my blood has eternal life, and I will raise him on the last day" (John 6:54). It is called a celebration because, through it, Christ gives us all the grace necessary for us to join Him, the Father, and the Holy Spirit in the joy of eternal live. It is one of the greatest gifts of His mercy toward us.

Activity

A. Show your children pictures of their Baptism and tell them that a holy oil called the oil of catechumens was rubbed on their chest with the Sign of the Cross. This oil is a sign of strength, a gift from God to guide them and guard them on every step of their journey through life. A second holy oil, the oil of chrism, a mixture of olive oil and balsam, was rubbed on the crown of their head. It is a sign of sealing with the gifts of the Holy Spirit. If you or your children have been confirmed, note that chrism oil is also used again in Confirmation.

B. Explain to your children that, on Holy Thursday, bishops in every diocese celebrate the Chrism Mass and bless three oils to be used throughout the year at parishes within their diocese. Your children were anointed at Baptism with two of these holy oils: the oil of catechumens and the chrism oil. The third holy oil is the oil of the sick. The anointing of the sick expresses healing and comfort.

C. Finally, share with your children some of the information you read about the Sacrament of the Anointing of the Sick, then help them complete **Signs and Symbols of the Sacrament (page 108 in the children's activity book)**.

Answers:

3   An anointing on the forehead symbolizes the need to know and follow Christ.

4   When sick people are anointed on the hands, they are reminded that they must turn all their activity over to Christ.

1   Sacramental oil symbolizes healing from illness, cleansing from sins, and consecration (setting apart as holy) by God.

5   This brings the comforting power of God to the sick person through the priest or bishop. The laying of the hands intends to communicate comfort, care, and concern.

2   The priest or bishop anoints the sick person's head or palm with the Sign of the Cross, uniting the suffering of the sick with the suffering of Jesus on the Cross.

The Effects of Anointing of the Sick
DISCUSSION AND CROSSWORD PUZZLE

Age level: Ages 8 and up

Recommended time: 10 minutes

What you need: The Effects of Anointing of the Sick (**page 109** in the children's activity book)

What you need to know before you begin:

The effects of Anointing of the Sick are:

> It gives the grace of "strengthening, peace and courage to overcome the difficulties that go with the condition of serious illness or the frailty of old age" (CCC 1520) and strengthens against discouragement and fear.

> It unites sick persons with the Passion of Jesus Christ and consecrates their suffering for participation in the saving work of Christ.

> If the person is too sick to receive the Sacrament of Penance, his sins are forgiven in the anointing.

> The anointing heals sick persons physically if that is best for their soul (CCC 1532).

> It is a preparation for the sick person's final journey home.

In the Sacrament of Anointing of the Sick, God shows His love for us. This activity explains one of the many ways in which Jesus loves and provides for us through this Sacrament. Encourage your children to read the effects of this Sacrament carefully, filling in the blanks with words from the word bank and complete the crossword puzzle.

Activity

Go over the effects of the Anointing of the Sick with your children, then work together to complete the crossword puzzle using words from the Word Bank.

Across

1. grace
2. forgiven
3. strengthens

Down

1. journey
2. salvation
3. unifies

 Connection to the Catechism

The special grace of the sacrament of the Anointing of the Sick has as its effects:

> - the uniting of the sick person to the passion of Christ, for his own good and that of the whole Church;
> - the strengthening, peace, and courage to endure in a Christian manner the sufferings of illness or old age;
> - the forgiveness of sins, if the sick person was not able to obtain it through the sacrament of Penance;
> - the restoration of health, if it is conducive to the salvation of his soul;
> - the preparation for passing over to eternal life. (CCC 1532)

BONUS ACTIVITY

How Can I Help?

Age level: All ages

Recommended Time: 20 minutes

What you need: How Can I Help? (**page 111** in the children's activity book)

Activity

A. Read what Jesus says about doing Corporal Works of Mercy in Matthew 25:34–40. In these verse, Jesus reminds us that helping sick people in any way is an act of love. Jesus tells us very clearly that when we help a suffering person, we are helping Him.

B. Use the scenarios on **How Can I Help? (page 111 in the children's activity book)** to spark discussion and brainstorming about helping those in need.

C. Encourage your children to pray for, reach out to, and remember the sick and the dying in your family, in your parish, and in your community. Talk about the importance of having compassion for those whose lives are challenged by illness. Discuss ways you can reach out to these people and help them. Together make a list of things you can do or have done in the past for others in need. Your list may include:

- Baking cookies
- Doing laundry and other household tasks
- Making a meal
- Shoveling a driveway
- Mowing a lawn
- Visiting
- Driving someone to an appointment
- Making a card
- Praying

D. Remind them that the Sacrament of Anointing of the Sick brings comfort to people who are suffering. When we pray, reach out, and remember the sick in our community, we bring them comfort and healing.

The Good Samaritan, by David Teniers the younger after Francesco Bassano.

Connection to the Catechism

Jesus'... compassion toward all who suffer goes so far that he identifies himself with them: "I was sick and you visited me." His preferential love for the sick has not ceased through the centuries to draw the very special attention of Christians toward all those who suffer in body and soul. It is the source of tireless efforts to comfort them. (CCC 1503)

The works of mercy are charitable actions by which we come to the aid of our neighbor in his spiritual and bodily necessities. ...The corporal works of mercy consist especially in feeding the hungry, sheltering the homeless, clothing the naked, visiting the sick and imprisoned, and burying the dead. (CCC 2447)

ACTIVITY 6

The Oil of Anointing
GRACE PERSON ACTIVITY

Age level: All ages

Recommended time: 5 minutes

What you need: Your Grace Person, Anointing of the Sick Symbol (**page 113** in the children's activity book), crayons or colored pencils, glue stick

Activity

A. After you have completed all the other activities this month, remind your children that the Sacrament of Anointing of the Sick consists essentially of the anointing of the head and the hands of the sick person with oil and the liturgical prayer that goes along with it (CCC 1531). (Some parishes have the sacred oils on display in a repository called an ambry. You may wish to see if you can locate the ambry in your parish!)

B. Ask your children to tell you all the other things they can remember that they have learned about this Sacrament.

C. After you have discussed the Sacrament, cut out the **Anointing of the Sick Symbol (page 113 in the children's activity book).** Have your children color the image, cut it out, and paste it on their Grace Person.

LESSON 11
THE TRIDUUM

Activities and Key Concepts

Activities you will do with your children	Key concepts the activity will teach	Recommended age and time
The Triduum: The Holiest Days of the Year	The Triduum begins with evening Mass on Holy Thursday and ends with Evening Prayer on Easter Sunday.	**Ages:** All ages **Time:** 20 minutes
Holy Thursday: Evening Mass of the Lord's Supper	On this night we celebrate the Institution of the Eucharist and Holy Orders, as well as the worth Christ gave to humble service.	**Ages:** All ages **Time:** 20 minutes
Good Friday: Celebration of the Lord's Passion	Good Friday is a day of mourning in which every Christian is left to ponder the gift of love that Jesus has given us in His Passion and Death.	**Ages:** All ages **Time:** 20 minutes
Holy Saturday: Vigil of the Lord's Resurrection	The Easter Vigil is the greatest celebration in the entire Church year.	**Ages:** All ages **Time:** 20 minutes

PART I

The Triduum: The Holiest Days of the Year

Age level: All ages
Recommended time: 20 minutes
What you need: What is the Triduum? reading

Activity

Read the information that follows aloud to your children, pausing to explain as needed to help younger children understand.

NOTE If possible, attend the Triduum celebrations of Holy Thursday Mass, Veneration of the Cross on Good Friday, and the Easter Vigil. You may also attend adoration after Holy Thursday Mass, or Stations of the Cross on Good Friday. Most schools do not object to children staying home on these holy days, or to their being released early to attend religious services. Short activity options are provided for each day of the Triduum if you are unable to attend the liturgical celebrations.

What is the Triduum?

*"We proclaim your death, O Lord, and profess your
Resurrection until you came again."*

The Paschal Triduum, taken from the Latin word meaning "three days," refers to the three days during which we celebrate the greatest mysteries of our Catholic Faith. It is the holiest season of the Church year. The Triduum begins with the evening Mass of the Lord's Supper on Holy Thursday, and ends with Evening Prayer (from the Liturgy of the Hours) on Easter Sunday, when we enter into the fifty days of Easter time. These three days are not days of Lent; the Lenten season ends with the beginning of the Pascal Triduum. Rather, these three days are set apart as a celebration of their own.

The Paschal Triduum consists of three major celebrations: the Mass of the Lord's Supper (Holy Thursday), the celebration of the Lord's Passion (Good Friday), and the Vigil of the Lord's Resurrection (Holy Saturday). We are invited during these holiest days to set this time apart in intense preparation for the celebration of the Easter Vigil, which is the climax of the Paschal Triduum. These days should be, as far as possible, free of entertainment, and free of work. We should continue our Good Friday fast until the Easter Vigil. This should be a time in which we reflect, pray, and wait. We want to arrive hungry and eager to celebrate as we begin the Easter Vigil.

Attend as many of the services the Church celebrates during these three days as you can. If you are able to participate in each service, you will taste, see, and hear the magnificent unfolding of the story of our salvation. During these days, we remember the institution of the Holy Eucharist and of Holy Orders, the Passion and death of Jesus Christ, and His glorious Resurrection from the dead. We also are caught up in the joyful hope of the final coming of Christ at the end of time. This Pascal Triduum is the center of the prayer of the Church. Let us join with her in praying and celebrating the mystery of our salvation!

PART II

Holy Thursday: Evening Mass of the Lord's Supper

Age level: All ages
Recommended time: 20 minutes
What you will need: Mass of the Lord's Supper reading

Activity

Read the information that follows aloud to your children, pausing to explain as needed to help younger children understand.

Mass of the Lord's Supper

The Evening Mass of the Lord's Supper ushers in the Paschal Triduum. It begins after sundown, as did the Passover Meal celebrated by Jesus. This service is second only to the Easter Vigil in importance in the Church year. On this night, we celebrate the institution of the Eucharist, when Jesus gave His Apostles His Body and Blood in anticipation of His death on the Cross the next day. In this action, Jesus showed His friends how He would win salvation for the entire world, and how He would continue to offer the graces He won on the Cross to all people, for all generations. This celebration was the first Mass.

At the Last Supper, Jesus instituted not only the Holy Eucharist but also the Sacrament of Holy Orders when He commanded His Apostles, "Do this in remembrance of me" (1 Corinthians 11:24). Jesus gave these men the power to continue to re-present this same sacrifice every time Mass is celebrated. The Apostles thus became the first priests.

During the Evening Mass of the Lord's Supper, we also see the worth that Jesus gave to humble service and the need to be washed with water, as we witness the Mandatum, or the washing of feet.

In the account of the Last Supper in John 13:5-15, we see how important it was for Jesus to communicate to His Apostles the need to serve one another in humility. "If I, therefore, the master and teacher, have washed your feet, you ought to wash one another's feet." This message was intended not only for the Apostles gathered in that room but to all who desire to follow Christ. Humble service is the hallmark of a Christian.

We see also in the washing with water great symbolism for the need of Baptism. Jesus said to Peter, "Unless I wash you, you will have no inheritance with me."

We must be "born again" in Baptism if we want to share in Christ's salvation.

Washing with water implies cleansing, which is where the traditional name for this day, Maundy Thursday, comes from. We see this cleansing also symbolized during the liturgy in the stripping of the altar and its washing with water.

On Holy Thursday, the Church consecrates many hosts to meet the need of all present at the Mass of the Lord's Supper as well as to distribute to all those who will attend services on Good Friday, when no Mass will be celebrated. This night, the Mass ends in silence and with the procession of the Blessed Sacrament to its place of repose. Everyone is invited to spend time in adoration of the Blessed Sacrament after Mass and into the night. This reminds us of how the disciples stayed and prayed with Jesus during His agony in the garden. When adoration is over, the Blessed Sacrament is reposed in a place where it will stay until Communion is distributed on Good Friday. This night, we remember that Jesus submitted Himself entirely to His Father's plan as He prayed, "Not my will but yours be done" (Luke 22:42). As one leaves the church, if the Blessed Sacrament is still exposed, it is proper to genuflect on both knees, with a bow, before the Blessed Sacrament.

BONUS ACTIVITY
Activities for Holy Thursday

Age level: All ages

A. In your home prayer space, read with your children the account of the Last Supper found in Luke 22:7-20 or any of the Gospel accounts of the events that happened on the first Holy Thursday. Then close with a prayer in thanksgiving for the Eucharist and the priesthood. Pray especially for your parish priest(s) and consider writing them a note or drawing them a picture, thanking them for being good servants.

B. Explain to your children that the Jewish people would thoroughly clean their home according to Jewish law in order to be ready to celebrate the Passover. This ritual of washing, or cleansing, brought forth the idea of spring cleaning that we have today. Have everyone work together to "spring clean" the house or their rooms in anticipation of Easter.

C. Read with your children the account of Jesus' agony in the garden from Luke 22:39-46. If possible, attend a holy hour as a family during the day, or attend adoration after the Holy Thursday celebration. If not, spend some time in prayer and "watching" with Jesus. Tell your children that when we stay with Jesus, we make reparation, or make up, for the time the Apostles fell asleep in the Garden of Gethsemane.

D. Observe the suggested fast with young children (who are not required to fast) by giving up dessert or eating only a simple meal. Explain to your children that fasting not only connects us more closely to God but makes us yearn for the things that we have fasted from. Easter candy always tastes better when we have gone without sweets for a while!

PART III

Good Friday: Celebration of the Lord's Passion

Age level: All ages
Recommended time: 20 minutes
What you will need: Good Friday reading

Activity

Read the information that follows aloud to your children, pausing to explain as needed to help younger children understand.

Good Friday

*"Save us, Savior of the world, for by your cross
and Resurrection you have set us free."*

The focus on Good Friday is the Cross of Jesus Christ. It is the day when the altar is bare, the door to the empty tabernacle is left open, and the Mass is not celebrated. The holy water fonts are empty. There is no need to genuflect when you enter church on this day. A slight bow before the altar is all that is proper. The Church is solemn and quiet. It is a day to meditate on the humiliation, pain, and suffering that Christ endured in order to save us. It is a day of mourning in which every Christian is left to ponder the magnificent gift of love that Jesus has given us in His Passion and Death. Of all days, this should be one of prayer, fasting, and penance.

This is the only day of the year when Mass is not celebrated, leaving us with a great sense of loss. It is the day in which the sinless Savior of the world gave His life for all. It is the day when His friends laid Him in a tomb. Somber and sad, the organ and the bells in the church are not heard. They are silent now until the great Alleluia of the Easter Vigil. Christ has died, and we meditate on this mystery and seek to enter into its truth.

One of the ways we meditate on the Passion of Christ is by praying the Way, or Stations of the Cross. In it, we remember the betrayal and the Passion of Jesus as He made His way to Calvary. We also realize that it was also our sins that nailed Him to the Cross. We pray to die to sin in our lives so that we may be united with Christ in His victory over sin.

The liturgy of Good Friday is the Celebration of the Lord's Passion. It is not Mass, because the Consecration does not take place, but the format of this liturgy does parallel that of Mass. It is divided into four sections:

> ‣ Liturgy of the Word – reading of the Passion
> ‣ Intercessory prayers for the Church and the world
> ‣ Veneration of the Cross of Jesus Christ
> ‣ Communion of the consecrated hosts

The Veneration of the Cross takes place after the Liturgy of the Word and the intercessions. A cross is placed in the front of the church, the priest or deacon chants, "This is the wood of the cross, on which hung the Savior of the world," and the congregation answers, "Come let us worship." Then everyone comes forward in a line to venerate (show great respect and honor to) the Cross in turn. This can be done by genuflecting or kneeling before the Cross and showing some form of respect and love, such as a touch or a kiss. The Cross of Jesus cannot be separated from His sacrifice, and thus in venerating the Cross we are adoring the Savior.

Crucifixion, by Anthony van Dyck.

After the Veneration of the Cross comes Communion. The priest brings out the ciborium (a large chalice used to store consecrated hosts) from the place of repose and places it on the altar while all stand in silence. The Our Father is prayed, and Communion is distributed. Final prayers are said, and all leave the church in silence, continuing to ponder the great mystery of Christ's death. The altar is then stripped. The Church remains now in silent prayer until the Easter Vigil.

BONUS ACTIVITY
Activities for Good Friday

Age level: All ages

A. Hold your own Veneration of the Cross at home. Light a candle in your home prayer space and bring out a cross or a crucifix. Have your family process to the cross and genuflect and kiss it. In a prayerful way, sign one another with the cross as a reminder of the price Jesus paid for your salvation. Then place the cross in a place where it will be seen by all, and leave it there until Holy Saturday evening.

B. Together with your children, keep holy the three hours when Christ hung on the Cross, traditionally thought of as from noon until three o'clock. If your children are old enough, observe silence and spend the time in prayer and devotional reading. Turn off phones. Turn off the TV, the computer, and so forth. Have your younger children place a favorite toy that they will give up playing with for the day (or for the three hours) next to the cross in your prayer space or in another prominent place.

C. Have every person in your family choose an unpleasant job or chore to do—a chore postponed or an activity usually avoided. Remind your children to unite the suffering or unpleasantness they feel with the suffering of Jesus on the Cross. When we unite our suffering with Jesus', we actually console Him. We are like Simon of Cyrene—we help Jesus carry His Cross!

PART IV

Holy Saturday: Vigil of the Lord's Resurrection

Age Level: All ages

Recommended time: 20 minutes

What you will need: Holy Saturday reading

Activity:

Read the information that follows aloud to your children, pausing to explain as needed to help younger children understand.

Holy Saturday

"Rejoice, heavenly powers! Sing, choirs of angels! Exult, all creation around God's throne! Jesus Christ, our King, is risen!"

Holy Saturday is the day of the Lord's rest, during which He lay in His tomb. For this reason, no Mass is said today until the evening Vigil. We wait quietly and prayerfully in the tension between darkness and light, between death and life. We ponder the mystery of salvation that is soon to be completed in the Resurrection of Jesus Christ.

At last, the long-awaited hour comes, and we are immersed in the Mother of all Holy Vigils, the Great Service of Light, the Paschal Vigil. This celebration is the greatest in the entire Church year. This night we celebrate Christ's passage from death to life. The Easter Vigil begins in darkness to symbolize His death. New fire is kindled and the Easter candle, which will be lit for all Baptisms throughout the year, is lit from this fire. The lit Paschal candle, symbolizing the Light of Christ, is brought by procession into the church, which is in darkness. All present have individual candles that are lit from the Paschal candle until the church is filled with light. As the candle moves forward toward the altar the priest or deacon sings three times "Christ our light," to which we all respond, "Thanks be to God." Then all of the lights in the church are turned on, and all present are bathed in light – the Light of Christ. This is followed by the Easter proclamation, known as the Exsultet, which ends part one of the Vigil, the Service of Light.

Part two of the Paschal Vigil is the Liturgy of the Word, in which two to seven readings from the Old Testament are read. These specially chosen passages tell the story of salvation history and how God prepared a people to accept the coming Savior, Jesus Christ. We are reminded of the great saving deeds that God performed for His people, from the creation of the world, to the Exodus from Egypt, and to the words of God spoken through the prophets. After each reading, we pause and respond to the Word of God in a psalm response. After the last reading, the altar candles are lit, and the Gloria is sung for the first time since the beginning of Lent. The bells are rung, and the organ is played. This is a time of great jubilation and praise to our God! A reading from Romans reminds us that we were baptized into Christ's death so that we might rise to new life in Him. The Gospel, taken from Luke, recounts the women finding Christ's tomb empty on Easter morning. The angel says to them, "Why do you search for the Living One among the dead? He is not here; he has been raised up."

The third part of the Paschal Vigil is the celebration of Baptism and Confirmation, the renewal of baptismal promises, and the reception of those seeking full communion with the Church. It begins by asking all to pray for the candidates for Baptism (the elect), and it includes a sung Litany of the Saints in which the saints' intercession is invoked. The water that will be used for the Baptisms is blessed. This water is a sign of the cleansing that takes place in the souls of those who will be baptized and is a reminder to all of their own baptismal cleansing. The elect are asked to renounce sin and profess their faith. They are then baptized and anointed with oil if they will not be confirmed. They are clothed with a baptismal garment and presented with a lit candle to symbolize the light of Christ that has come to them. Everyone, including the candidates for full reception into the Church, then renews their baptismal promises while holding a lit candle. This is followed by a profession of faith for all who will be received into the Church, and then all the candidates who are in need of the Sacrament of Confirmation are confirmed.

The Mass continues with the intercessions. The Church is now ablaze not only with Easter light, but with Easter joy. The music is rich and full; the responses should be loud and heartfelt, for Christ our Savior has passed over from death to life. "He is not here. He has been raised up."

BONUS ACTIVITY
Activities for Holy Saturday

Age level: All ages

A. Have your children color or decorate Easter eggs. Eggs have long been a symbol for the Resurrection. Like the chick that bursts forth from the egg, so too did Christ burst forth from the tomb of death to new life. Death had no hold on Him. Consider decorating your eggs with Christian symbols, such as a cross, or words, such as Alleluia.

B. Read together with your children some of the great Scripture stories that will be read at the Vigil, or have your children tell you some of the ones that they know. Have your children act out the readings: assign parts and have your children read them dramatically, or act as you read.

C. Have a Vigil celebration with your children at home. It is possible to buy Easter candles that are made for family use and can be reused year after year. These candles can be lit on baptismal days for your family and on Easter itself, as well as during the Easter season. Light the Easter candle as a symbol of darkness turned into light with the light of Christ.

NOTE However you choose to celebrate this great event, make rich use of the symbols of light and water. Recall Baptism and birth into new life. Rejoice in song and with Alleluias. Christ our Savior is risen indeed!

Connection to the Catechism

Beginning with the Easter Triduum as its source of light, the new age of the Resurrection fills the whole liturgical year with its brilliance. Gradually, on either side of this source, the year is transfigured by the liturgy. (CCC 1168)

St. Bernadette

SAINT OF THE MONTH

Age level: All ages

Recommended time: 10 minutes

What you need: St. Bernadette (**page 115** in the children's activity book), markers and/or crayons

Activity

Read aloud the story of this month's saint to your children. You may also want to show them the full page saint image. While you are reading or sometime the next day, have them complete the coloring page on **page 117** in the children's activity book.

Biography of St. Bernadette

BERNADETTE SOUBIROUS was born in France, the eldest of nine children. Her family was poor, and had to live in a single basement room that used to be a jail. Ever since she was little, Bernadette suffered from bad health and severe asthma, a disease that affects the lungs and makes it difficult to breathe. Because she often had to stay home sick, Bernadette could barely read and write.

On February 11, 1858, when she was 14, Bernadette went to gather wood on the bank of a river near a natural grotto or cave. As she was taking off her shoes to cross a stream, she heard a rustling like the wind. The trees and the river were completely still. Only the bushes near the grotto were moving. There she saw, in a niche above the trees, a Lady of about her height.

The Lady was very beautiful, all dressed in white, with a blue girdle about her waist, and a long rosary hanging over her arm. She gestured for Bernadette to pray, and together they prayed the Rosary.

Bernadette continued to visit the grotto, and large crowds of people came to watch her, even though they could not see the Lady. They made fun of Bernadette and thought she was crazy. During one of her visits, the Lady instructed Bernadette to drink from a spring near the grotto. Bernadette could find nothing but muddy water and had to scratch at the dirt in order to drink. The crowds laughed at Bernadette's muddy face, but were amazed to find that later in the day the water had turned into a clear spring of water that ran into the river. People flocked to the spring. A man who had been blind for 20 years washed his eyes with the water and was healed! Another lady brought her sick child to the spring, and he also was healed. Many, many miracles happened at the spring.

The Lady appeared to Bernadette a total of 18 times and requested that a chapel be built near the grotto. When Bernadette asked the Lady who she was, the Lady responded, "I am the Immaculate Conception," revealing that she was the Blessed Virgin Mary.

In 1866, Bernadette joined the sisters of Notre-Dame de Nevers and took care of the sick people in the infirmary. She became sick herself, but never went to the spring for healing. Bernadette saw her suffering as something she could offer up to God.

Bernadette died at 35 years of age and is a great example of patient suffering. Today a great shrine to the Blessed Virgin Mary is built above the spring she found. The water was channeled into a place where people can bathe in it and receive healing. Many people from all over the world travel to this shrine every day to be healed.

Bernadette Soubirous was canonized in 1933 and is the patron saint of the sick. Her feast day is on April 16.

BONUS ACTIVITY
Praying with St. Bernadette

Age level: All ages
Recommended Time: 15 minutes
What you need: Praying with St. Bernadette (**page 118** in the children's activity book)

Explain that praying for the sick is always good. The World Day of the Sick is a special day when we are called to pray for everyone suffering with illnesses. Pope St. John Paul II chose for this day February 11, the feast of Our Lady of Lourdes, who appeared to St. Bernadette in 1858. He explained that this day should be "a special time of prayer and sharing, of offering one's suffering for the good of the Church, and of reminding us to see in our sick brother and sister the face of Christ." Follow the directions on **Praying with St. Bernadette (page 118 in the children's activity book)** to pray a litany for the sick and suffering people you know, as well as those who care for them.

March in Review

THIS MONTH YOU EXPLORED AS A FAMILY THE QUESTIONS:

What is Anointing of the Sick?

How does this Sacrament affect us?

What are the liturgical celebrations of the Triduum?

In Lesson 10 your children learned:

› Jesus told the Apostles to heal the sick in His name.

› Our suffering can be redemptive if we unite it to Christ's.

In Lesson 11 your children learned:

› The Triduum begins with evening Mass on Holy Thursday and ends with Evening Prayer on Easter Sunday.

› The Easter Vigil is the greatest celebration in the entire Church year.

In this space below, write some reflections about the past month. What was your favorite activity? What didn't go as well? Will you adjust anything about what you're doing? What special intentions do you have for next month?

MY NOTES

April
OVERVIEW

VERSE OF THE MONTH
MARK 10:43-45

Whoever wishes to be great among you will be your servant; whoever wishes to be first among you will be the slave of all. For the Son of Man did not come to be served but to serve and to give his life as a ransom for many.

SAINT OF THE MONTH
ST. GIANNA BERETTA MOLLA

LESSON 12
HOLY ORDERS

Overview

In this lesson we learn about the Sacrament of Holy Orders, one of the sacraments directed toward the service of others. The Sacrament of Holy Orders is the continuation of Christ's priesthood, which He bestowed upon His Apostles. We will come to understand the three orders of this Sacrament; the signs and effects of the Sacrament; and the form and minister of the Sacrament of Holy Orders.

Catechism Articles to Read

› 1572–1600

Words to Know

› Holy Orders
› Degrees of Holy Orders
› Consecration

LESSON 13
HOLY MATRIMONY

Overview

In this lesson we learn about the Sacrament of Matrimony in which a baptized man and woman are joined together in a holy covenant. Christ raised this covenant to a Sacrament in which the couple receives grace to love one another as Christ loves the Church: permanently, faithfully, and fruitfully. We will come to understand the signs and effects and the form and minister of the Sacrament of Matrimony.

Catechism Articles to Read

> 1601-1666

Words to Know

> Marriage

BY THE END OF THIS MONTH, YOUR CHILDREN SHOULD BE ABLE TO:

- ✔ Recite this month's Scripture Passage

- ✔ Define this month's Words to Know

- ✔ Explain the Sacrament of Holy Orders

- ✔ Explain the Sacrament of Matrimony

- ✔ Explain how these two Sacraments are fulfilled in service

- ✔ Tell you about St. Gianna Beretta Molla

YOUR
Catholic Home
PRAYER CARDS

Prayer cards are a wonderful way to introduce your children to the Communion of Saints! Each card typically has an image of a saint, our Lord, or the Blessed Virgin on one side and, on the other, a prayer associated with that particular image.

The first prayer cards were sold as keepsakes to pilgrims in the Middle Ages to commemorate their visit to some holy site or shrine. Since then, the popularity of prayer cards has endured as they are reminders of our friends in heaven.

Practice It!

Find prayer cards of your children's patron saints, or patrons of activities that your children are involved in; for example, St. Cecilia is the patron saint of musicians, St. Sebastian of athletes, and Sts. Gemma Galgani and Thomas Aquinas of students. Place saints you are particularly devoted to in your home prayer space. For the rest, get a binder where your children can collect and even trade prayer cards with the other children of your parish community.

Celebrate!

ST. GIANNA MOLLA
APRIL 28

Our task is to live holy the present moment.
—*St. Gianna Molla*

THINGS TO DO THIS MONTH:

1 Pray together that each person in the family may be open to the vocation that God has planned for him or her.

2 The Feast day of St. Mark is April 25. Look up pictures of Saint Mark's Basilica in Venice, Italy, and find out why the basilica was named after him.

VERSE OF THE MONTH
MARK 10:43-45

"Whoever wishes to be great among you will be your servant; whoever wishes to be first among you will be the slave of all. For the Son of Man did not come to be served but to serve and to give his life as a ransom for many."

REMEMBER!
From the very beginning of creation it is clear that the vocation of marriage was part of God's original plan.

MEMORIZE! Holy Orders is the sacrament through which the mission entrusted by Christ to his apostles continues to be exercised in the church until the end of time: thus it is the sacrament of apostolic ministry. (CCC 1536)

ST. GIANNA BERETTA MOLLA

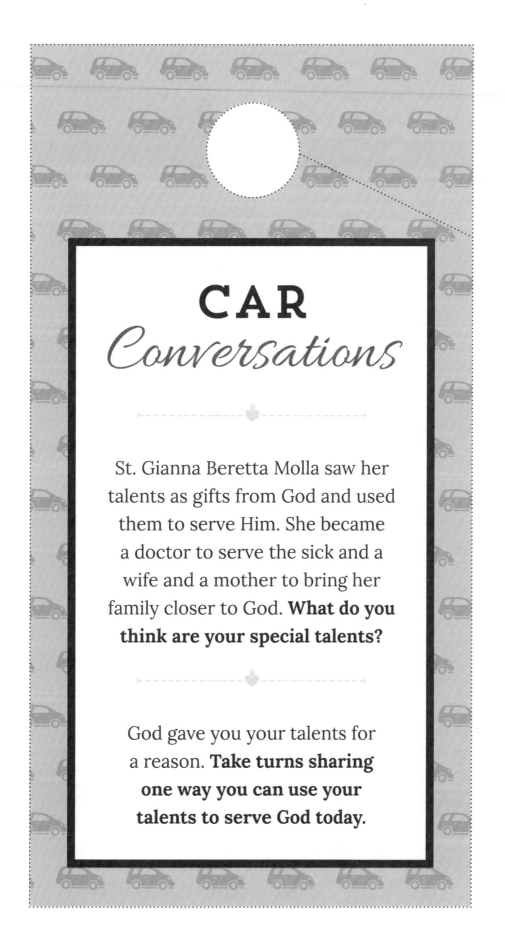

CAR
Conversations

St. Gianna Beretta Molla saw her talents as gifts from God and used them to serve Him. She became a doctor to serve the sick and a wife and a mother to bring her family closer to God. **What do you think are your special talents?**

God gave you your talents for a reason. **Take turns sharing one way you can use your talents to serve God today.**

LESSON 12
HOLY ORDERS

Activities and Key Concepts

Activities you will do with your children	Key concepts the activity will teach	Recommended age and time
What Is the Sacrament of Holy Orders? Reading and discussion	Jesus continues His ministry through His priests.	**Ages:** All ages **Time:** 10 minutes
The Lord Is My Shepherd Scripture reading and reflection	Our bishops and priests lead us in faith and show us the way to Heaven.	**Ages:** All ages **Time:** 10 minutes
The Sacrament of Holy Orders Prefigured Scripture analysis	By making a sacrifice of bread and wine instead of a bloody animal sacrifice, Melchizedek prefigures Jesus Christ.	**Ages:** Ages 10 and up **Time:** 15 minutes
The Sacrament of Holy Orders Began with Jesus Christ Creative activity and Scripture analysis	Jesus called the Apostles to be His first priests.	**Ages:** All ages **Time:** 15 minutes
The Degrees of Holy Orders Discussion and word search	The degrees of Holy Orders are bishops, priests, and deacons.	**Ages:** All ages **Time:** 10 minutes
The Call of the Priest Grace Person activity	Review of the rite of Holy Orders and the duties of priests.	**Ages:** All ages **Time:** 5 minutes

WORDS TO KNOW

The Words to Know are words that you and your children should know and understand at the end of this month. Use your best judgment about which words to expect each of your children to learn. For older children, you may want to have them create flashcards to help them remember what they have learned.

Holy Orders	The sacrament by which a man is consecrated in Christ's name to continue the apostolic ministry.
Degrees of Holy Orders	There are three degrees of Holy Orders: episcopate (bishop), presbyterate (priest), diaconate (deacon).
Consecration	The dedication of a thing or a person to divine service by a prayer or a blessing.

Please choose from the activities for the month.

It is not necessary to complete every activity. We offer a wealth of activities to choose from because each child learns differently, so select the activities that best suit the learning needs of you family. Feel free to shorten or improvise on each activity as necessary. You know best what your family needs!

ACTIVITY 1

What Is the Sacrament of Holy Orders?
READING AND DISCUSSION

Age level: All ages

Recommended time: 10 minutes

What you need: The Sacrament of Holy Orders (**page 124** in the children's activity book)

Discussion

A. Read the essay on the Sacrament of Holy Orders on the next page.

B. Next, discuss the the essay as a family. For younger children, go over the main points at a level that they will understand. For older children, you may have them read the essay themselves, then discuss with them what they read. The essay is also in the children's activity book on **page 124.**

C. Make sure to discuss the following points:

  › Jesus carries on His ministry in the Church through His priests.

  › Priests do not act under their own authority. Their authority comes from Jesus.

  › This Sacrament includes three "degrees" or roles in the Church: bishops, priests, and deacons.

D. Ask your children to think of the priests and deacons they know, or who they see at your parish. How do they serve you and others in the parish and community? What would be missing in your life if these men had not been called by God to continue His work?

E. Have a discussion about the gift that the priests, deacons, and bishop are to your family. List some specific ways they touch your life. As a family how can we appreciate and support our priests, deacons and Bishop? For example:

   › Pray for our pastor

   › Volunteer at our parish

   › Support funds for retired priests

   › Pray for the Pope

   › Follow the Pope's teachings and prayers through Catholic Media

F. Together, brainstorm other concrete actions we will take to honor those who serve us in the Sacrament of Holy Orders.

Prayer

Close by leading your family in the following prayer composed by Pope Francis:

Lord of the Harvest, bless young people with the gift of courage to respond to your call. Open their hearts to great ideals, to great things. Inspire all of your disciples to mutual love and giving – for vocations blossom in the good soil of faithful people. Instill those in religious life, parish ministries, and families with the confidence and grace to invite others to embrace the bold and noble path of a life consecrated to you. Unite us to Jesus through prayer and sacrament, so that we may cooperate with you in building your reign of mercy and truth, of justice and peace. Amen.

The Sacrament of Holy Orders Essay

Christ promised that He would never leave us or forsake us (Hebrews 13:5), and that He would not leave us as orphans (John 14:18). Have you ever wondered how He fulfills these promises now that He has ascended into Heaven? One way is through the Sacrament of Holy Orders.

Jesus knows that we are both physical and spiritual beings, so in the Sacraments He addresses both the physical and spiritual aspects of our nature. Along those lines, in Holy Orders He approaches us in the person of the priest – a human being we can see, hear, and touch.

The Priesthood of All Believers

The bible tells us that every baptized Christian shares in what is called the Common (or Universal) Priesthood of believers: "But you are 'a chosen race, a royal priesthood, a holy nation, a people of his [God's] own'" (1 Peter 2:9a).

Christ has given the laity the right and duty to participate in His priesthood through our active participation in the Mass, Confession, prayer, and almsgiving. This participation also includes the witness of our life as we practice both self-denial and charity. In order to fulfill this mission we need the graces of the Sacraments and the teachings of the Church, which is where Holy Orders comes in.

Holy Orders

Christ calls some men to teach, strengthen, and guide His children (the Church) by providing the Sacraments and performing particular types of service in His place. The Sacrament of Holy Orders is the Sacrament in which those men are consecrated in Christ's name to continue the mission that was "entrusted by Christ to his apostles ... until the end of time" (CCC 1536). It includes three degrees: episcopate (bishops), presbyterate (priests), and diaconate (deacons). It is also known as: the Sacrament of the Ministerial Priesthood, the Sacrament of Ordained Priesthood, the Sacrament of Apostolic Ministry, and it is a Sacrament at the Service of Communion.

While the priesthood is a great and necessary gift to the Church, it does not mean that the ordained minister is free from personal weaknesses or even from sin. But the Sacrament of Holy Orders does guarantee that the grace of the Sacraments is valid and effective even when they are performed by a sinful minister. Why? Because it is truly Christ who is the minister of grace through the Sacraments.

Not only is it Christ who works through the ordained minister, but it is Christ who calls men to that ministry. The *Catechism of the Catholic Church* teaches: "No one has a right to receive the Sacrament of Holy Orders. Indeed no one claims this office for himself; he is called to it by God. ...Like every grace this sacrament can be received only as an unmerited gift" (1578). A call to the Sacrament of Holy Orders is a call to serve. The ministerial priesthood is at the service of the Common Priesthood of all believers in the Church.

 Connection to the Catechism

Holy Orders is the sacrament through which the mission entrusted by Christ to his apostles continues to be exercised in the Church until the end of time: thus it is the sacrament of apostolic ministry. It includes three degrees: episcopate, presbyterate, and diaconate. (CCC 1536)

ACTIVITY 2

The Lord Is My Shepherd
SCRIPTURE READING AND REFLECTION

Age level: All ages
Recommended time: 10 minutes
What you need: Bible, The Lord is My Shepherd (**page 126** in the children's activity book)

The Good Shepherd stained glass, St John the Baptist's Anglican Church, Ashfield, New South Wales.

What you need to know before you begin:

God loves and provides for all our physical and spiritual needs. As members of the Church, we are all sheep in God's flock. From Heaven God is watching over us and protecting us and on earth His shepherds, our priests and bishops, are teaching and guiding us. Our priests and bishops lead us in faith and show us the way to Heaven. The shepherd of the whole Church is the pope.

Jesus is also our Good Shepherd and we are his sheep. Jesus said, "I will lay down my life for the sheep" (John 10:15). Jesus died for us so that we may have forgiveness of sins and life everlasting. Christ wants each of us to become fully mature and complete in Him so that we can enter into His joy. For this reason He has given His Church the gift of Holy Orders through which we receive the Sacraments, learn His teachings, and are shepherded (led and governed) by Him.

Activity

A. Read aloud Psalm 23 found on **The Lord is My Shepherd (page 126 in the children's activity book)**. Explain that it is a song about God's love for us.

B. As you read, ask your children to imagine the places David describes. Imagine they are part of the scene. What do you see? What do you hear? What can you smell, taste, or touch?

C. Connect the Psalm to the priesthood. Jesus continues His ministry through the priesthood. Through His priests, Jesus shepherds believers (leads and governs us).

BONUS ACTIVITY
A Sheep in Jesus' Flock Craft

Age level: Ages 5-8
What you need: Blank paper, glue, google eyes, cotton balls

Draw a large sheep on a piece of blank paper. Have your children write at the top of the page: "Psalm 23" and "The Lord is my shepherd" (or as much of the Psalm as they would like to copy onto the page). Then glue on google eyes and cotton balls. Help your child think of ways they can be a good sheep in Jesus' flock, and have them write their ideas on the page around the sheep.

The Sacrament of Holy Orders Prefigured
SCRIPTURE ANALYSIS

Age level: Ages 10 and up

Recommended time: 15 minutes

What you need: Who is Melchizedek? (**page 127** in the children's activity book)

Melchizedek Offering Bread and Wine to Abraham, by Giovanni Battista Franco.

Activity

A. Like all the Sacraments, Holy Orders is prefigured in the Old Testament. Ask your children if they have heard the name Melchizedek at Holy Mass. If they can't remember hearing his name in the Mass, tell them that he is mentioned in *The Eucharistic prayer during Mass*:

> Be pleased to look upon these offerings with a serene and kindly countenance, and to accept them, as you were pleased to accept the gifts of your servant Abel the just, the sacrifice of Abraham, our father in faith, and the offering of your high priest Melchizedek, a holy sacrifice, a spotless victim.

B. Have them turn to **Who is Melchizedek? (page 127 in the children's activity book)** and read about Abram's encounter with Melchizedek in Genesis 14:18-20:

> Melchizedek, king of Salem, brought out bread and wine. He was a priest of God Most High. He blessed Abram with these words: "Blessed be Abram by God Most High, the creator of heaven and earth; And blessed be God Most High, who delivered your foes into your hand." Then Abram gave him a tenth of everything.

C. Have your children complete the questions in the activity book, then go over the answers together.

Answers:

1. Who is Melchizedek? *Melchizedek was a king and high priest during the time of Abram.*

2. What did Melchizedek do when he met Abram (Abraham)? *Melchizedek offered him bread and wine, and then gave him a blessing.*

3. How was Melchizedek's offering different from other offerings in Genesis (refer to Genesis 15:7-12)? *Melchizedek offered bread and wine, not a blood sacrifice which was the custom of the time.*

4. What was the significance of Melchizedek's actions? *By making a sacrifice of bread and wine instead of a bloody animal sacrifice, Melchizedek prefigures or points to Jesus Christ.*

5. How was the offering made by Melchizedek similar to the offering made by your priest during the Liturgy of the Eucharist? *Melchizedek did not offer a bloody sacrifice, but gave bread and wine. His actions are the same as the Eucharistic Celebration: worshippers give their offerings and Jesus works through the priest and gives His body and blood in the bread and wine.*

 Connection to the Catechism

The Christian tradition considers Melchizedek, priest of God Most High, as a prefiguration of the priesthood of Christ, the unique high priest after the order of Melchizedek holy, blameless, unstained, by a single offering he has perfected for all time those who are sanctified, that is, by the unique sacrifice of the cross. (CCC 1544)

ACTIVITY 4

The Sacrament of Holy Orders Began with Jesus Christ
CREATIVE ACTIVITY AND SCRIPTURE ANALYSIS

Age level: All ages, with one activity for children ages 5-8 and another for children ages 8 and up

Recommended time: 15 minutes

What you need: Bible, Come and Follow Me (**page 129** in the children's activity book), The Sacrament of Holy Orders Began with Jesus Christ (**page 132** in the children's activity book)

What you need to know before you begin:

The Sacrament of Holy Orders began with Jesus Christ when He gave His Apostles the sacred power to serve the people of God by offering the Sacrifice of the Mass, forgiving sins, healing the sick, and baptizing in His name.

Activity for Children Ages 5-8

A. Explain that Jesus called His first priest, the Apostles, by saying to them, "Come and follow me!" Today many men also hear God's call to priesthood.

B. Have your children color the pictures on **Come and Follow Me (page 129 in the children's activity book)** as you read the information with each image:

> **Come and Follow Me:** Jesus called His first priest, the Apostles, by saying to them, "Come and follow me!" These men followed Jesus from town to town listening to His sermons, witnessing His miracles, and praying with Him often. Jesus made these faithful men priests, giving them the power to forgive sins, celebrate Mass, and serve His people.

Christ Calling the Apostles James and John. by Edward Armitage.

- **Who Hears God's Call?:** Today Jesus continues to call baptized men to be priests. When these men hear God's call they go to a seminary, a place where men prepare to be priests, to learn how to celebrate Mass, forgive sins, help the dying, and to serve God's people. They also pray and talk to God.

- **The Grace of the Holy Spirit:** Jesus made St. Peter the head of the Apostles and of His Church. Saint Peter was the first pope and the Apostles were the first bishops. St. Peter and the Apostles ordained many priests. Today bishops take the place of the Apostles and by the power of God they ordain our priests. The bishop, while laying his hands on the young man, prays to God asking to grant the ordinand, the man preparing to be a priest, the graces of the Holy Spirit to minister to his flock in the name of Jesus.

- **A Priest Forever:** Jesus came to show us the way to Heaven. Jesus wants our priest to guide us and lead us to Heaven. Imagine the joy in a young priest's heart the first time he forgives someone their sins, the first time he changes the bread and wine into the Body and Blood of Jesus, and the first time he anoints someone who is dying, preparing them for Heaven. Our priests love Jesus with all their hearts and they are called to share Jesus' love with us.

Activity for Children Ages 8 and Up

Ask your older children to turn to **The Sacrament of Holy Orders Began with Jesus Christ (page 132 in the children's activity book)**. Have them find each Scripture passage in their Bibles, read the verse, then write a brief summary explaining which of the sacred powers of the priest Jesus is giving to his Apostles. Each verse is a biblical reference to the priesthood.

Answers:

> **Matthew 28:16, 18-20:** "The eleven disciples went to Galilee ... Jesus approached and said to them, 'All power in heaven and on earth has been given to me. Go, therefore, and make disciples of all nations, baptizing them in the name of the Father, and of the Son, and of the holy Spirit, teaching them to observe all that I have commanded you. And behold, I am with you always, until the end of the age.'" *Baptism.*

> **John 20:21-23:** "[Jesus] said to them again, 'Peace be with you. As the Father has sent me, so I send you.' And when he had said this, he breathed on them and said to them, 'Receive the holy Spirit. Whose sins you forgive are forgiven them, and whose sins you retain are retained.'" *Forgiving sins.*

> **Matthew 10:7-8:** "[Jesus said,] 'The kingdom of heaven is at hand. Cure the sick, raise the dead, cleanse lepers, drive out demons.'" *Healing the sick.*

> **1 Corinthians 11:24-25:** "and, after he had given thanks, broke it and said, 'This is my body that is for you. Do this in remembrance of me.' In the same way also the cup, after supper, saying, 'This cup is the new covenant in my blood. Do this, as often as you drink it, in remembrance of me.'" *The Sacrifice of the Mass.*

 Connection to the Catechism

The chosen people was constituted by God as "a kingdom of priests and a holy nation." But within the people of Israel, God chose one of the twelve tribes, that of Levi, and set it apart for liturgical service; God himself is its inheritance. A special rite consecrated the beginnings of the priesthood of the Old Covenant. The priests are "appointed to act on behalf of men in relation to God, to offer gifts and sacrifices for sins." (CCC 1539)

ACTIVITY 5

The Degrees of Holy Orders
DISCUSSION AND WORD SEARCH

Age level: All ages
Recommended time: 10 minutes
What you need: Holy Orders (**page 134** in the children's activity book)

What you need to know before you begin:

The three degrees of the Sacrament of Holy Orders are: bishops (the episcopate), priests (the presbyterate), and deacons (the diaconate). All three degrees are conferred by the same Sacrament of Holy Orders.

We can trace the unbroken line of apostolic succession through the bishops. The bishop, in the fullest sense possible, serves in the place of Christ as teacher, shepherd, and priest. Only the bishop can administer the Sacrament of Holy Orders, and he is normally the one who administers the Sacrament of Confirmation. The bishop has care over the particular Church given to him by the Pope, and is "responsible with the other bishops for the apostolic mission of the Church" (CCC 1560). Only the Pope can ordain a person to be a bishop.

In order to fulfill their mission across the many churches and institutions within a diocese, bishops ordain local priests to assist with some of their ministerial duties. "Priests can exercise their ministry only in dependence on the bishop and in communion with him" (CCC 1567). From their bishop they receive charge over a parish community or a particular ecclesial office.

The priest is the ordinary minister of the Sacraments other than Confirmation and Holy Orders. Because of his administration of the Sacraments the priestly office is sometimes referred to as the office of "sanctification" as distinguished from the bishop's office of teaching and governing.

At the third Degree of Holy Orders are the deacons who are ordained for a ministry of service. The deacon is ordained by his local bishop and is assigned his specific ministry of service by him. A deacon may serve at the celebration of the Sacraments, especially the Eucharist. He may also distribute Holy Communion, bless marriages, baptize, preside over funerals, proclaim the Gospel and preach, and dedicate himself to various charitable ministries.

The Sacrament of Holy Orders leaves an indelible spiritual character that cannot be repeated or removed. The vocation and mission received on the day of ordination is a permanent mark. This activity will explain the gifts each candidate of the three degrees of Holy Orders (deacon, priest, or bishop) receives in the Sacrament of Holy Orders from the Holy Spirit.

The ordination of a bishop, a priest, or a deacon is an important event in the Church. The celebration usually takes place during the Eucharistic Liturgy on a Sunday, in a Cathedral, with many faithful witnesses in attendance. Ordination to the priesthood requires holiness of life, moral integrity, and celibacy.

Activity

A. Have your children turn to **Holy Orders (page 134 in the children's activity book)** and read the information. For younger children, you may wish to read the information aloud to them. Discuss with your children anything they may not understand, and share any additional details from the information you read before the lesson.

B. Next, have your children complete the Word Search. Quiz them on terms of the degrees of Holy Orders when they are finished.

BONUS ACTIVITY
Priest Interview

Age level: All ages

Have you children ask your pastor's permission to conduct a brief interview. As priests are often overworked, be understanding if he cannot spare the time. If he agrees, have your children prepare good and relevant questions beforehand. Prompt their thinking with the following: How do you think your priest spends his day? What struggles or obstacles did he overcome to become a priest? How is God moving in his priesthood now? After the interview, have your child write your priest a letter thanking him for answering God's call.

ACTIVITY 6

The Call of the Priest
GRACE PERSON ACTIVITY

Age level: all ages
Recommended time: 5 minutes
What you need: Colored pencil or marker, piece of solid cloth if you wish to cut out a stole

Activity

A. Explain to your children that the bishop anoints the priest's hands with oil when the priest is being ordained. He prays that Jesus may preserve the priest so that he can sanctify the Christian people and offer sacrifice to God.

B. In the Old Testament, priests were anointed with oil to signal that they were being set apart to perform a sacred duty. When the newly ordained priest's hands are anointed, it signifies that his hands are being prepared for the sacred duties of his priestly ministry. He can now offer up the Eucharist, anoint the sick and the dying, and give a priestly blessing, among other things.

C. Draw a cross on each hand of your grace person to represent the sacred duties a priest performs with his hands.

D. You may also create a stole, the band of cloth the priest wears around his neck, for your grace person to wear. Cut out from solid cloth a long rectangular piece resembling a scarf and hang it around your grace person so that the two ends are dangling in the front. Alternatively, you can cut out long rectangular pieces of construction paper and tape them together to make an even longer piece. Make sure you choose a color from the liturgical calendar: red, green, white, purple, or rose.

Connection to the Catechism

The bishop receives the fullness of the sacrament of Holy Orders, which integrates him into the episcopal college and makes him the visible head of the particular Church entrusted to him. As successors of the apostles and members of the college, the bishops share in the apostolic responsibility and mission of the whole Church under the authority of the Pope, successor of St. Peter. (CCC 1594)

Priests are united with the bishops in sacerdotal dignity and at the same time depend on them in the exercise of their pastoral functions; they are called to be the bishops' prudent co-workers. They form around their bishop the presbyterium which bears responsibility with him for the particular Church. They receive from the bishop the charge of a parish community or a determinate ecclesial office (CCC 1595).

Deacons are ministers ordained for tasks of service of the Church; they do not receive the ministerial priesthood, but ordination confers on them important functions in the ministry of the word, divine worship, pastoral governance, and the service of charity, tasks which they must carry out under the pastoral authority of their bishop. (CCC 1596)

The sacrament of Holy Orders is conferred by the laying on of hands followed by a solemn prayer of consecration asking God to grant the ordinand the graces of the Holy Spirit required for his ministry. Ordination imprints an indelible sacramental character. (CCC 1597)

LESSON 13

HOLY MATRIMONY

Activities and Key Concepts

Activities you will do with your children	Key concepts the activity will teach	Recommended age and time
Marriage in the Plan of God Video and discussion	Marriage is not man's idea, it is God's plan. Marital love reflects divine love.	**Ages:** All ages **Time:** 10 minutes
Jesus Made Marriage a Sacrament Family art and Scripture reflection	Original Sin damaged the communion between God and man, as well as between husband and wife. Jesus redeemed both	**Ages:** Ages 8 and up **Time:** 10 minutes
The Rite of Marriage Reading of wedding vows	The exchange of consent between the couple makes the marriage. The Holy Spirit seals their covenant.	**Ages:** All ages **Time:** 25 minutes
Love Is Patient, Love Is Kind Family scripture reflection	Marriage creates a bond that lasts as long as the spouses live.	**Ages:** All ages **Time:** 10 minutes
There Are Three in a Marriage Grace Person activity	Jesus is the center of marriage and the family.	**Ages:** All ages **Time:** 5 minutes

LESSON 13
WORDS TO KNOW

The Words to Know are words that you and your children should know and understand at the end of this month. Use your best judgment about which words to expect each of your children to learn. For older children, you may want to have them create flashcards to help them remember what they have learned.

Marriage	The Sacrament by which a man and a woman enter into a lifetime commitment of covenanted love.

ACTIVITY 1

Marriage in the Plan of God
VIDEO AND DISCUSSION

Age level: All ages
Recommended time: 10 minutes
What you need: Sophia SketchPad Marriage video found at **SophiaSketchPad.org**, unlined paper, colored pencils or crayons

What you need to know before you begin:

At the very beginning of creation God made it clear that marriage was a part of His original plan and that He is its author: "God created mankind in his image; in the image of God he created them; male and female he created them" (Gen 1:27).

God, who is love, created man and woman in His image for love. Thus, the God-given vocation of every human being is to love. And in a unique way man and woman were created for each other and called to become one in a covenant of love: "The Lord God said: 'It is not good for the man to be alone.' ... The Lord God then built the rib that he had taken from the man into a woman. When he brought her to the man, the man said: 'This one, at last, is bone of my bones and flesh of my flesh; This one shall be called "woman."' ... That is why a man leaves his father and mother and clings to his wife, and the two of them become one body" (Gen 2:18-24). This oneness becomes an image of the absolute and unfailing love that God has for us. After God created man and woman He said to them, "Be fertile and multiply; fill the earth and subdue it" (Gen 1:28).

From the very first chapters of Scripture we see that God created man and woman in His image and called them to love. He created them for each other and joined them together in a covenant of love (marriage) and oneness that cannot be broken. This covenant is to be "fruitful" and its work is to watch over creation and to partake in procreation.

Activity

A. Together, watch the Sophia Sketchpad Marriage video at **SophiaSketchPad.org**.

B. Ask your children what parts of the video they liked best, and what questions it raised in their minds.

C. Finish by having your children draw on their own paper an original icon or representation for how marriage reflects the Blessed Trinity.

NOTE You can acknowledge that it is true that many marriages fail. This does not mean the spouses are bad people. But their marriage fell short of the ideal God intended for them. Even if a couple decides they can no longer live together, they are still husband and wife in the eyes of God.

Connection to the Catechism

The matrimonial covenant, by which a man and a woman establish between themselves a partnership of the whole of life, is by its nature ordered toward the good of the spouses and the procreation and education of offspring; this covenant between baptized persons has been raised by Christ the Lord to the dignity of a sacrament. (CCC 1601)

ACTIVITY 2

Jesus Made Marriage a Sacrament
FAMILY ART AND SCRIPTURE REFLECTION

Age level: Ages 8 and up

Recommended time: 10 minutes

What you need: The Bible Begins and Ends with a Wedding (**page 136** in the children's activity book)

The Wedding Feast at Cana, by Julius Schnorr von Carolsfeld.

What you need to know before you begin:

As the *Catechism* makes clear, God created marriage for the good of the spouses: "The acts in marriage by which the intimate ... union of the spouses takes place ... are noble and honorable; the truly human performance of these acts fosters the self-giving they signify and enriches the spouses in joy and gratitude. Sexuality is a source of joy and pleasure. ...The Creator himself ... established that in the [generative] function, spouses should experience pleasure and enjoyment of body and spirit" (CCC 2362).

God's creation was perfect and the union of man and woman in marriage was complete. Then came sin. Since original sin, marriage has been "threatened by discord, a spirit of domination, infidelity, jealousy, and conflicts that can escalate into hatred and separation" (CCC 1606). To return to God's plan, man and woman need the help of God's grace. "Without his help man and woman cannot achieve the union of their lives for which God created them 'in the beginning'" (CCC 1608).

By applying the fruit of His Cross, Jesus raised marriage to a Sacrament – Matrimony. This Sacrament is a source of great grace for all baptized persons who receive it and is one of the ways God provides spouses with the graces necessary to live their marriage according to His original plan.

Activity

A. Explain to your children that sacramental marriage is a covenant: a sacred promise that creates family bonds. Marriage has existed since God made it when He created Adam and Eve.

B. The first consequence of the Fall was a rupture of communion between Heaven and earth, and in the communion between husband and wife. Marriage existed even after the Fall because it is in our natures. But until Jesus came, it was not a Sacrament.

C. Have your children turn to **The Bible Begins and Ends with a Wedding (page 136 in the children's activity book)**. Explain that now that Jesus has redeemed us and made marriage a Sacrament, marriage too reflects God's divine nature. We can read the Bible to see that Salvation History begins and ends with a wedding:

  › In the beginning, the first people God created were Adam and Eve: the first married couple.

  › When Jesus came, He first revealed Himself to the public as the Son of God and Savior in the midst of a wedding. By doing so, Jesus announced that the time has come for God's relationship with His people to be restored at the same time that He elevated marriage to a Sacrament. And just as Jesus was present at the Wedding at Cana, He gives husbands and wives the graces and the strength to live the Sacrament of Matrimony as a Sacrament of love.

  › Finally, Scripture concludes with a vision of the wedding feast of the lamb in the Book of Revelation.

D. Next, have them look at each piece of art and answer the questions that follow.

The Creation of Eve, Orthodox icon.

The Adoration of the Lamb (detail from the Ghent Altarpiece), by Jan van Eyck.

1. **Creation of Adam and Eve, Orthodox icon:** Read Genesis 2:22-24. How does the icon Creation of Adam and Eve help you understand these verses? *Accept reasoned answers.*

2. **The Wedding Feast at Cana, by Julius Schnorr von Carolsfeld:** Read the Gospel story of the Wedding at Cana in John 2:1-12. What moment in the Gospel story has the artist captured? How does the painting help you better understand the story of the Wedding at Cana? *Accept reasoned answers.*

3. **The Adoration of the Lamb (detail from the Ghent Altarpiece), by Jan van Eyck:** Read Revelation 19:7-9. Who is the bride of the Lamb? *The Church.*

4. Do these words sound familiar? "Blessed are those who have been called to the wedding feast of the Lamb." Where have you heard them before? *These words are said by the priest just before Communion at each Holy Mass.*

 Connection to the Catechism

Sacred Scripture begins with the creation of man and woman in the image and likeness of God and concludes with a vision of the wedding feast of the Lamb. Scripture speaks throughout of marriage and its mystery, its institution and the meaning God has given it, its origin and its end, its various realizations throughout the history of salvation, the difficulties arising from sin and its renewal in the Lord in the New Covenant of Christ and the Church. (CCC 1602)

The Rite of Marriage
READING OF WEDDING VOWS

Age level: All ages

Recommended time: 25 minutes

What you need: The text of the Rite of Marriage from **SophiaOnline.org/RiteofMarriage**

What you need to know before you begin:

Although a marriage covenant must be witnessed to by an authorized Church authority, it is the exchange of consent between the couple that makes the marriage. For a marriage to be valid it must have the following elements:

> The couple must be free to marry (they must be of opposite sexes, not already be married, nor be close relatives etc.).

> They must freely consent to the marriage and not be under constraint.

> In consenting to marry, they must have the intention to marry for life, to be faithful to one another, and to be open to children.

> Their consent must be given in the presence of two witnesses and before a properly authorized Church minister.

The consent consists of the act of the couple giving themselves to one another as expressed in the words of the marriage vows: "I take you to be my wife" and "I take you to be my husband."

Activity

A. Encourage your children to design invitations to invite guests to a reading of the Celebration of the Rite of Marriage. This activity will give couples an opportunity to renew their vows as well as expose your children to the marriage rite.

B. Have a married couple read aloud the Rite, available at **SophiaOnline.org/RiteofMarriage**.

C. Afterwards, explain to your children that the Sacrament of Holy Matrimony is the act of a couple committing to each other so that the two become one.

D. Ask your children to tell you about their favorite part of the Rite or which part was the most meaningful to them.

BONUS ACTIVITY
The Celebration of Marriage

Age level: Ages 5-8
What you need: The Celebration of Marriage (**page 139** in the children's activity book), markers and/or crayons

---

Ask your younger children to turn to **The Celebration of Marriage (page 139 in the children's activity book),** and while they color the picture, read the information aloud to them:

> The Eucharist is the memorial of how Christ gave His life for His bride, the Church. How appropriate that as a Christian couple commit their lives to one another in the Mass, they unite their offering to one another with Christ's offering made present in the Eucharist!

 Connection to the Catechism

The various liturgies abound in prayers of blessing and epiclesis asking God's grace and blessing on the new couple, especially the bride. In the epiclesis of this sacrament the spouses receive the Holy Spirit as the communion of love of Christ and the Church. The Holy Spirit is the seal of their covenant, the ever available source of their love and the strength to renew their fidelity. (CCC 1624)

Love Is Patient, Love Is Kind
FAMILY SCRIPTURE REFLECTION

Age level: All ages
Recommended time: 10 minutes
What you need: Bible

What you need to know before you begin:

In the Sacrament of Matrimony a man and a woman consecrate themselves to be committed to one another until death. This means they promise to be true to each other and love one another in a special way for the rest of their lives. A married couple also promises to raise children who are a beautiful gift from God.

Marriage is a vocation which is not simply a personal preference or a state of life to be lived, but rather a call from God. Men and women are called to the vocation of matrimony for their joy and good, and for the procreation and education of children. The Church teaches clearly that "Parents are the principal and first educators of their children. In this sense the fundamental task of marriage and family is to be at the service of life" (CCC 1653).

The very nature of marriage where "they are no longer two, but one flesh" implies a unity and indissolubility (Matthew 19:6). This mutual self-giving is strengthened by the grace of the Sacrament of Matrimony and deepened by the couple's life of common faith and the Eucharist.

The Church teaches that "Children are the supreme gift of marriage and contribute greatly to the good of the parents themselves" (CCC 1652). As parents, we have a duty to educate our children, as well as to respect and encourage their vocations. May all the graces necessary to fulfill this solemn obligation be ours in Jesus Christ!

Discussion

A. Share with your children stories of married couples you admire and try to name specific ways each couple shares and contributes to their married lives; for example, helping each other, praying together, doing kind things for each other, and raising a family together.

B. Read together 1 Corinthians 13:4-7:

> Love is patient, love is kind. It is not jealous, [love] is not pompous, it is not inflated, it is not rude, it does not seek its own interests, it is not quick-tempered, it does not brood over injury, it does not rejoice over wrongdoing but rejoices with the truth. It bears all things, believes all things, hopes all things, endures all things.

C. Emphasize that marriage isn't always easy and that lasting marriages take work. Love is not a "feeling" we can fall in and out of. Love is a choice we freely make. Both people in a marriage must make a choice every day to love their spouse, even if they feel like they don't want to. They each have to make sacrifices, to forgive each other, and set aside time together to talk, laugh, and share their lives.

D. Conclude by answering together the following question: How can a married couple be a sign of Jesus' presence in our world?

NOTE You can acknowledge that it is true that many marriages fail. This does not mean the spouses are bad people. But their marriage fell short of the ideal God intended for them. Even if a couple decides they can no longer live together, they are still husband and wife in the eyes of God.

 ### Connection to the Catechism

Yet there are some situations in which living together becomes practically impossible for a variety of reasons. In such cases the Church permits the physical separation of the couple and their living apart. The spouses do not cease to be husband and wife before God and so are not free to contract a new union. In this difficult situation, the best solution would be, if possible, reconciliation. The Christian community is called to help these persons live out their situation in a Christian manner and in fidelity to their marriage bond which remains indissoluble. (CCC 1649)

BONUS ACTIVITY
Card Making Activity

Age level: all ages
Recommended time: 10 minutes
What you need: Unlined paper or card stock, colored pencils, any photographs, artwork, photos from magazines, and so forth.

A. Remind your children that God calls all of us to love and serve others. Some people are called to be priests or religious. These people give their lives to the Church. God calls some people to be holy by being married. Husbands and wives give their lives to each other. Through the Sacrament of Matrimony, they promise to accept the gift of children from God and to help each other and their families get to Heaven.

B. Help your children create a list of married couples who are each a great example of Christian marriage. They can be relatives, couples from your parish, or from your community. Make and decorate a card for each couple, thanking them for their example, and letting them know they are in your prayers.

C. Close with a prayer for each couple that they will receive God's graces with an open heart.

 Connection to the Catechism

[Christian spouses] have their own special gifts in the People of God. This grace proper to the sacrament of Matrimony is intended to perfect the couple's love and to strengthen their indissoluble unity. (CCC 1641)

ACTIVITY 5

There Are Three in a Marriage
GRACE PERSON ACTIVITY

Age level: all ages
Recommended time: 5 minutes
What you need: Marriage Symbol (**page 140** in the children's activity book)

Activity:

A. Explain to your children that it is the free consent of the couple that makes the Sacrament of Matrimony. But, because of sin and the Fall, human beings are selfish. It is very easy for each person in the marriage to put him or herself before the other and no longer be self-giving. That is why Jesus must always be part of the marriage. Jesus' grace through the Sacrament is what allows the couple to keep their marriage promises to each other. This is another reason why praying together as a family is so important. Praying together reminds everyone that Jesus is at the center of the family and of the marriage.

B. Cut out and have your children color **Marriage Symbol (page 140 in the children's activity book)** while you explain the symbol:

   › The interlocking wedding rings are a sign of never-ending love because a circle is never-ending, and the rings are interlocked because the couple is one flesh.

   › The monogram at the center of the rings is called a *Chi Rho* and is a symbol for Christ. It comes from the first two letters of the Greek word for Christ, *Christos*, the chi (X) and the rho (P).

C. When your children are finished coloring in the image, have them cut it out and paste it on their Grace Person.

St. Gianna Molla
SAINT OF THE MONTH

Age level: All ages
Recommended time: 10 minutes
What you need: St. Gianna Beretta Molla (**page 141** in the children's activity book), markers and/or crayons

Activity

Read aloud the story of this month's saint to your children. You may also want to show them the full page saint image. While you are reading or sometime the next day, have them complete the coloring on **page 141** in the children's activity book.

Biography of St. Gianna Molla

GIANNA BERETTA MOLLA was born October 4, 1922, in Italy, the tenth of thirteen children. Her family was very devout and passed on to Gianna the gift of the Catholic faith. Together as a family they prayed the daily rosary, attended daily mass, and consecrated themselves to the Sacred Heart.

As a child, Gianna spent much time outdoors, and loved to go hiking and skiing. She also felt a special call to serve others, and was very active in her Catholic Youth community and did volunteer work to take care of the poor through the St. Vincent de Paul Society. Her call to serve others was so strong that she went to medical school to become a doctor. When she opened her own doctor's clinic, she was most drawn to serve mothers,

children, the poor, and the elderly. Gianna viewed her practice of medicine as a mission from God.

After much prayer, Gianna realized that she was called to the vocation of marriage. She wanted to create a Christian family where her children could learn to love God and become holy. She married Pietro Molla, a Catholic engineer, and had three children. The happy couple called their children their "treasures." When Gianna became pregnant a fourth time, the doctors discovered that Gianna had a deadly tumor in her uterus. To get rid of the tumor, the doctors gave Gianna three options: 1) She could have an abortion, 2) She could have a surgery that would also get rid of her child, or 3) The doctors could remove only the tumor and save the life of her child, but that would make giving birth dangerous. Gianna was a strong Catholic and a doctor dedicated to saving lives. She knew that the life of her unborn child was sacred and precious to God. She bravely chose to only remove the tumor and save the life of her child.

When the time came for Gianna to give birth, she heroically told the doctors to save her child's life over her own if they had to. She gave birth to a healthy baby girl and was so happy to see her!

Sadly, Gianna died a week later due to complications from her pregnancy even though the doctors tried very hard to save her.

Gianna Beretta Molla was canonized on May 16, 2004 and stands as a witness to life and the importance of family. Pietro Molla attended her canonization and is the first husband to attend the canonization of his wife. Gianna's feast day is on April 28, and she is the patron saint of mothers, physicians, and unborn children.

Connection to the Catechism

God who created man out of love also calls him to love the fundamental and innate vocation of every human being. For man is created in the image and likeness of God who is himself love. Since God created him man and woman, their mutual love becomes an image of the absolute and unfailing love with which God loves man. It is good, very good, in the Creator's eyes. And this love which God blesses is intended to be fruitful and to be realized in the common work of watching over creation." (CCC 1604)

April in Review

THIS MONTH YOU EXPLORED AS A FAMILY THE QUESTIONS:

What does God call each of us to do?

How do bishops, priests, and deacons continue Christ's ministry?

What is a sacramental marriage?

In Lesson 12 your children learned:

- Christ brings His ministry to us through called men who receive Holy Orders.

- Our bishops and priests lead us in faith and show us the way to Heaven.

In Lesson 13 your children learned:

- In the Sacrament of Marriage, a man and a woman enter into a lifetime commitment of covenanted love.

- The exchange of consent between the couple makes the marriage. The Holy Spirit seals their covenant.

In this space below, write some reflections about the past month. What was your favorite activity? What didn't go as well?

ESSAY APPENDIX

The following essays offer you a complete catechesis on the month's topic by presenting the content from learning activities into one or two readings. You may use these essays at the adult meetings to guide your conversations in response to the discussion questions.

GOD IS THE SOURCE OF ALL LIFE

BACKGROUND READING

God is the Creator of all things, both visible and invisible, which He created out of nothing. This doctrine of creation reveals important truths about the nature of God, creation, and human beings. God reveals these truths that we cannot see through the things we can see — material creation — using signs and symbols. First among these is the Church, the visible sign of God's communion with humanity. Jesus established His Church to make known the Kingdom of God on Earth and to gather all people to Him so that we might know God's love and be saved from sin and death.

Creator of All Things Visible and Invisible

The book of Genesis opens with some of the most famous words in the Bible, "In the beginning, when God created the heavens and the earth…" The sacred author goes on to describe a formless and shapeless darkness covering an abyss, surrounded by primordial waters over which a mighty wind swept. And then God spoke: "Let there be light," and there was.

All of this poetic language explains what was present in the beginning — or, more precisely, before the beginning. Christians have long used the phrase "out of nothing," or *ex nihilo* in Latin, to describe this scene — what and how God created. God did not use any preexisting material to create the universe. The formlessness and shapelessness express the nothingness that was before the beginning, and the darkness and the abyss express the emptiness of the nothingness.

The wind that swept over the water in the sacred author's portrait of creation is recognized as the Spirit of God hovering over the nothingness. God made all things, the material and the spiritual, out of nothing, with only the power of His voice. Given this doctrine, we can understand the sacred author as saying that in the beginning, when God created all that is, visible and invisible, there was nothing but God Himself, who spoke creation into existence. All of creation, therefore, owes its existence to God.

We learn from the doctrine of creation that God is all powerful and all knowing, for nothing exists that did not come from Him. We learn that nature is real and not a mirage because it came from a Creator, that nature is fundamentally good, and that God reveals Himself to us through His creation. We learn that humanity has been given dominion over God's creation, that we have a fundamental dignity as human beings made in God's image and likeness, and that our purpose is to honor and glorify God in this life through the things He has made.

God Reveals Himself through His Creation

The invisible God communicates Himself to us through His visible creation. For example, we know love, an invisible reality, through physical signs and symbols – a hug, a gift, or spoken words.

Human beings are both body and soul, visible and invisible, material and spiritual. Out of love for us, the invisible, spiritual God became visible. Taking on human flesh, God became man in the Person of Jesus Christ, who was like us in all things but sin. We call this fundamental teaching of our Faith the Incarnation. Jesus Christ is God's love fully revealed.

Jesus communicates the Father's love for us in visible, physical ways, going so far as to give Himself completely to us, Body and Blood, Soul and Divinity, in the Eucharist, so that we might become one Body in Him. He gave His life and died on the Cross to save us from sin.

The Church: A Visible Sign of the Invisible Kingdom of God

Jesus established His Church here on Earth to continue His mission of the salvation of all souls. The Church is a visible sign of the invisible Kingdom of God, inaugurated by Christ during His earthly life.

The Church uses visible signs and symbols to make known the invisible truths of our salvation. These visible signs of God's love communicate His very life to us. We call this free and undeserved gift of God's life *grace*. Grace is necessary for us to persevere on the path of holiness, to avoid sin, and ultimately to attain Heaven. In His divine wisdom, Jesus gave us the seven Sacraments as visible, material means of receiving the invisible grace of God.

How beautiful it is that God's grand design for His creation and for our salvation is made known to us still through the work of Christ's Church!

WHAT IS A SACRAMENT?

BACKGROUND READING

It is human nature to mark the movements of life with signs and traditions. God uses signs and traditions to make Himself known to us. Throughout human history, God has revealed Himself and made His love known to us using signs taken from creation and human culture. Jesus instituted seven very special signs, or Sacraments, not only to symbolize God's grace but *actually to confer it on us.*

The seven Sacraments are different from every other sign in the world because they bring about what they signify. For example, smoke is a sign of fire, but it does not cause fire. Baptism is a sign of rebirth, and it actually causes that rebirth. Confession is a sign of God' healing mercy, and it actually brings about that healing.

Signs and Symbols

Human beings have always used signs and symbols to communicate, to mark important moments in life, and to better understand invisible truths. God knows this is how we work. He created us, after all, and therefore, He made us this way. God,

from the very beginning, has made Himself known to us through signs and symbols that communicate His very nature and life. Although God is invisible to the eye, and transcends, or is beyond, His creation, He is present and near to us. We can recognize Him in His creation. Specifically, He gives us grace through physical signs and symbols. Grace is the free and undeserved gift of God's life in us. We must receive the grace of God in faith and use it to serve and glorify Him.

Salvation History

Throughout salvation history, God has made Himself known in specific ways, to prepare us, His people, for the gift of salvation. Salvation history is the story of God's saving actions in human history. God entered into a series of covenants with man by which He gradually and in stages, in words and deeds, revealed more of Himself and drew us deeper into relationship with Him. Each new covenant contained a sign, taken from human experience, to represent the depth of God's love present at the heart of each covenant. Marriage between a man and woman, the rainbow, circumcision, the Law, and the Temple all took on greater meaning in their communication of God's love and mercy.

Finally, at the appointed time, God Himself entered into human history by sending His only, beloved Son, the Second Person of the Blessed Trinity, to become human, like us in all things but sin. Jesus fully revealed the Father and communicated His grace to us in and through His life and teaching. He performed miracles as signs of God's love and mercy and to announce the coming of the Kingdom of God. And then He poured out His love for us by sacrificing Himself on the Cross, paying the debt of sin that we could not. By His Cross and Resurrection we are freed from sin and made holy. Our salvation has been won!

The Seven Sacraments

In this age of the Church, which Jesus Himself founded during His earthly life to carry on His mission of salvation of all souls, we continue in the tradition of our spiritual ancestors by recognizing certain signs and symbols as having the power to communicate God's love to us. The Seven Sacraments of the Church — Baptism, Confirmation, Holy Eucharist, Penance and Reconciliation, Anointing of the Sick, Holy Orders, and Holy Matrimony — all instituted by Christ, are efficacious signs of God's grace. This means that each Sacrament not only is a visible representation of God's love and life, but also effects, or causes, God's grace to be present. The Sacraments, in fact, are the primary means for us to receive grace, particularly by frequent reception of the Eucharist.

As advanced as we might be in our modern world, little has changed in respect to basic human experiences. We all are born to a mother and father. We all experience love and joy, sadness and fear. We all make mistakes and lose our way sometimes. We all experience sickness and suffering. Our lives are remarkably similar to those who lived thousands of years ago. And like our predecessors, we too mark the important moments of our lives with signs, symbols, rituals, and traditions. This is how we work. This is how God made us.

Jesus Christ instituted each Sacrament. He entrusted them to the Church to administer them to His people throughout the ages. God's grace is necessary for us to grow in holiness and get to Heaven. We cannot do either of those things by ourselves. Therefore, it is necessary for us to receive the Sacraments in order to receive God's grace.

Just as the blood of the Paschal Lamb on the doorposts of the Israelites in Egypt was a sign of life, the Sacraments are signs of God's life in us that fill us with His life and make us holy. The Sacraments fulfill God's actions in the Old Covenant, make present our salvation won by Christ on the Cross, and fill us with hope for eternal life with God in Heaven.

THE SACRAMENTS OF INITIATION

BACKGROUND READING

The Church has seven Sacraments: Baptism, Confirmation, Eucharist, Penance and Reconciliation, Anointing of the Sick, Holy Orders, and Holy Matrimony. Of those seven Sacraments, we recognize three as the Sacraments of Initiation because they introduce us to and make us members of the Church, strengthen us for our life's journey, and give us our vocation, or calling, as Christians.

To be initiated means formally to become a part of a group or society. In general, initiations may involve taking an oath, passing a challenge, or enduring a trial. Then upon initiation, the person has a common bond with other members and is given a role or mission. The Sacraments of Initiation resemble this pattern. The Christian life begins with baptismal promises, and then through God's grace we are made members of Christ's Body, the Church. We receive the mission shared by all disciples of Christ to become holy, and to bring the Good News to the world. In Confirmation our baptismal grace is perfected, and we receive a strengthening of the gifts of the Holy Spirit. In the Eucharist, the source and summit of the Christian life, we receive the very Body and Blood of Our Lord Jesus Christ, which nourishes us in our mission to evangelize. We will learn more about these Sacraments throughout the year.

The Catechism of the Catholic Church teaches us, "Baptism, Confirmation, and Eucharist are sacraments of Christian initiation. They ground the common vocation of all Christ's disciples, a vocation to holiness and to the mission of evangelizing the world. They confer the graces needed for the life according to the Spirit during this life as pilgrims on the march towards the homeland" (1533). In other words, the vocation of each Christian person is holiness and the mission of bringing the Gospel to every person in the world. The true home of a Christian is not earth but Heaven.

Our Vocation to Holiness

Jesus tells us in Matthew's Gospel: "So be perfect, just as your heavenly Father is perfect" (5:48). He tells us more about what that means in Matthew 22:37-39: "He said to him, 'You shall love the Lord, your God, with all your heart, with all your soul, and with all your mind. This is the greatest and the first commandment. The second is like it: You shall love your neighbor as yourself.'"

Jesus' saying from the second passage (Matthew 22:37-39) helps us to understand His saying from the first passage (Matthew 5:48). To be perfect as our heavenly Father is perfect means to love Him first above all else and to love our neighbors as ourselves.

We are all called to be holy. Because of the Sacraments of Initiation—Baptism, Confirmation, and the Eucharist—we are given the vocation of holiness that all of Jesus' disciples share, and we are strengthened by the Sacraments of Initiation to be able to attain that holiness. To be perfect as our Heavenly Father is perfect is to be holy. And Jesus then tells us how to be holy, which is to obey the two greatest commandments, to love God above all else, and to love our neighbor as ourselves. This is how we become saints.

Indeed, the lives of the saints give us powerful examples of how to be holy. The *Catechism* tells us "the holiness of the People of God will grow in fruitful abundance, as is clearly shown in the history of the Church through the lives of so many Saints" (CCC 2013).

The Mission to Evangelize

Pope Paul VI wrote that the Church "exists to evangelize." Evangelization is the sharing of the Gospel by word and example of life. Jesus Himself gave the Apostles this mission before He ascended into Heaven. "Then Jesus approached and said to them, 'All power in heaven and on earth has been given to me. Go, therefore, and make disciples of all nations, baptizing them in the name of the Father, and of the Son, and of the Holy Spirit, teaching them to observe all that I have commanded you. And behold, I am with you always, until the end of the age'" (Matthew 28:18-20). Evangelization is doing exactly what Jesus commanded His Apostles to do. The Sacraments of Initiation, as we've learned, give us the same vocation as all of Christ's disciples, which includes evangelization.

The word *evangelization* comes from the Latin word *evangelion*, which means "gospel." Our word *gospel* comes from the Greek word *eungelion* which means "good message" or "good news." Although we often use the word *gospel* to mean the four books of the Bible by Matthew, Mark, Luke, and John, the word has a much richer meaning. The gospel is the Good News of Jesus Christ: that He came down from Heaven, died for us on the Cross, and rose from the dead to offer us salvation. At its heart, the call to evangelization means we are called to share the Good News in our lives.

BAPTISM

BACKGROUND READING

The Catechism of the Catholic Church provides a simple explanation for what Jesus does for us in Baptism: "Holy Baptism is the basis of the whole Christian life, the gateway to life in the Spirit, and the door which gives access to the other sacraments. Through Baptism we are freed from sin and reborn as sons of God; we become members of Christ, are incorporated into the Church and made sharers in her mission: Baptism is the sacrament of regeneration through water in the word" (CCC 1213).

Baptism is necessary for salvation and has been prefigured throughout salvation history, to prepare for its institution by Christ's own Baptism and His command to His Apostles. By Baptism, we are made new creations, and with the support of the whole Christian community, we advance on the journey toward salvation.

Matter and Form

All Sacraments have matter and form. The matter is the physical material used. The form refers to the words that are spoken. In the Sacrament's most fundamental form, the minister of Baptism (ordinarily a priest) immerses the person being baptized three times in water (or pours water three times upon his head) while saying the words given to us by Jesus, "I baptize you in the name of the Father, and of the Son, and of the Holy Spirit" (see Matthew 28:19).

This bath in water spiritually cleanses the baptized, removing all sin from his soul, including the stain of Original Sin inherited from Adam and Eve. The sins of the baptized are removed, and sanctifying grace, the free and undeserved gift of God's very life, which is necessary for salvation, is conferred upon the soul. (However, the weakness of our fallen nature remains, and we are still prone to sin. This tendency to sin is called concupiscence.)

Baptism also initiates the baptized into the Church, serving as a communal rite of passage that bestows on the person all the rights and privileges – as well as all the responsibilities – that come with being a member of Christ's Church.

Baptism Instituted and Prefigured

Jesus Himself was baptized at the beginning of His public ministry, not because He needed to be, but because it was fitting that He be baptized, in order to serve as our model of holiness and to show us the way to salvation.

At the end of His earthly dwelling, as Matthew 28 tells us, Jesus commanded His Apostles to go to all the nations and make disciples of them, "baptizing them" in the Trinitarian formula we use today, and "teaching them to observe all" that He taught them. Jesus' Baptism and His commissioning of the Apostles to baptize are the culmination of thousands of years of preparation for the Sacrament, as God prefigured the Sacrament of Initiation throughout His saving work in salvation history.

From the very beginning, when the Spirit of God hovered over the primordial waters, to Noah and the Great Flood, to the crossing of the Red Sea and the River Jordan, we have always understood the signs that have pointed the way to Baptism. God's people pass from chaos, death, slavery, and sin, through powerful and life-giving waters, to new life in grace and freedom as a new creation.

The Fruits of Baptism

The sins of the baptized are forgiven and the gifts of the Holy Spirit are infused into their souls. The baptized are made new creatures in the sight of God, partakers of the divine nature and members of Christ Himself, co-heirs with Him to all God's promises. The baptized are made members of the Church and allowed access to all the other Sacraments by right and are tasked with a share in the mission of the Church: to share the Good News of the Gospel and make disciples of Jesus Christ. An indelible spiritual mark is also placed on the baptized person's soul, much like the mark a king makes in wax to seal a letter, ensuring the letter is his. No sin can remove this seal from the soul. It marks him forever as belonging to God, set apart for the day of redemption and eternal life with Him.

Baptism is a visible sign that effects what it signifies, as given to us directly by Christ. The graces of Baptism, nurtured by the whole Christian community, can bear much fruit and lead the baptized on the journey toward salvation.

CONFIRMATION

BACKGROUND READING

The Sacrament of Confirmation is often misunderstood, despite the rich history of the Sacrament that reaches back to Jesus and the Apostles and its deep roots in the Old Testament. Contrary to popular belief, it is not a graduation ceremony or the Catholic equivalent of a Jewish bar mitzvah. Rather, the Sacrament of Confirmation is an important step on the path of Christian initiation that completes, or confirms, the outpouring of the Holy Spirit received at Baptism and sends the person out to proclaim boldly the Good News. "By the sacrament of Confirmation, [the baptized] are more perfectly bound to the Church and are enriched with a special strength of the Holy Spirit. Hence they are, as true witnesses of Christ, more strictly obliged to spread and defend the faith by word and deed" (CCC 1285).

Confirmation in Salvation History

The roots of the Sacrament can be found throughout the Old Testament. From early on, God made known to His people what He desired for them: "You will be to me a kingdom of priests, a holy nation" (Exodus 19:6). God sought to make of His people a royal priesthood who would proclaim and glorify His name to all the nations and serve Him in love.

By the time Israel became a royal kingdom, it was already well established that priests and kings were anointed with holy oil as a symbol of consecration—that is, of being set apart as belonging to God—and as a symbol of the outpouring of God's Spirit upon them to commission them for God's service and to strengthen them for the work ahead according to their position. All of the kings in the line of David were anointed at their inauguration as king and became "messiahs" in Hebrew or "christs" in Greek, both of which mean "anointed one." Later, the prophets foretold of a day on which God would "pour out [His] spirit upon all flesh" (Joel 2:28).

Jesus, while completing His work of salvation, announced, "For on [the Son of Man] the Father, God, has set His seal" (John 6:27), proclaiming that He was the awaited Christ. Further, He promised to send the Holy Spirit, the Advocate, after Him to teach and to confirm all that has been revealed to us and to empower us to proclaim the Good News of salvation: "But you will receive power when the Holy

Spirit comes upon you, and you will be my witnesses in Jerusalem, throughout Judea and Samaria, and to the ends of the earth" (Acts 1:8). And on Pentecost, when the Blessed Virgin Mary and the Apostles had gathered in the Upper Room, with a rush of wind, the Holy Spirit descended upon them as tongues of fire and emboldened them to preach to the gathered crowd and soon to all the nations.

"Be Sealed with the Gift of the Holy Spirit"

The tradition of anointing with holy oil, or chrism, as a seal of the Holy Spirit continues in the Sacrament of Confirmation. The bishop, the ordinary minister of the Sacrament, speaks the words "Be sealed with the gift of the Holy Spirit" while laying his hands on the confirmand, signifying the outpouring of the Spirit in a succession of imposition of hands that stretches back to the Apostles. These words and actions bring to fruition God's desire for His people to be a royal priesthood. Indeed, Confirmation increases the gifts of the Holy Spirit within the person, and "gives [him] a special strength of the Holy Spirit to spread and defend the faith by word and action as true witnesses of Christ, to confess the name of Christ boldly, and never to be ashamed of the Cross" (CCC 1303).

The Sacrament of Confirmation uniquely gives us the fullness of the Christian mission as well as the ability and strength to complete it. In Confirmation we, as St. Paul proclaims, "put on the armor of God" and "hold faith as a shield, to quench all [the] flaming arrows of the evil one" (Ephesians 6:11, 16).

Who Can Receive Confirmation?

The Church teaches clearly that "Every baptized person not yet confirmed can and should receive the sacrament of Confirmation" (CCC 1306). In the early Church, Baptism and Confirmation were received together. Increasing numbers of infant Baptisms made it impossible for the bishop to be present for all of them, and for this and other reasons, the two began to be offered separately. In the Latin rite today, Confirmation is most commonly received after the recipient has attained the age of reason, with the age being set by the bishop. The Eastern Church, on the other hand, retained the tradition of offering Confirmation at the same time as Baptism. In this way the Eastern Church emphasizes the unity of Baptism and Confirmation.

To receive Confirmation, a baptized person "must profess the faith, be in the state of grace, have the intention of receiving the Sacrament, and be prepared to assume the role of disciple and witness to Christ," both in the Church and in the world (CCC 1319). A candidate for Confirmation should seek a practicing Catholic to serve as a sponsor, to be a model of faith and encouragement. Because of Confirmation's close connection to Baptism, it is desirable, if possible, that one of the baptismal godparents serve as the sponsor. It is also customary that the one to be confirmed chooses the name of a saint – someone who exemplifies to them a life of holiness – as a Confirmation name.

THE EUCHARIST: JESUS, THE PASSOVER LAMB

BACKGROUND READING

Our study of the Sacraments of Initiation culminates in the Eucharist. Although in many places the Sacrament of Confirmation is received after the first Holy Communion, the Church teaches clearly that "The holy Eucharist completes Christian initiation. Those who have been raised to the dignity of the royal priesthood by Baptism and configured more deeply to Christ by Confirmation participate with the whole community in the Lord's own sacrifice by means of the Eucharist" (CCC 1322).

The Catechism of the Catholic Church calls the Eucharist "the Sacrament of sacraments" (CCC 1330) and "the source and summit of the Christian life" (CCC 1324). All the other Sacraments and every ministry of the Church flow from the Eucharist and point us toward it. The reason for the centrality of the Eucharist is that the Eucharist is Christ Himself!

Jesus instituted the Eucharist at the Last Supper. In anticipation of His death on the Cross, Jesus gave His Apostles – whom He made the first priests – His Body and Blood to eat and drink. And because Jesus wanted all His people for all time to eat and drink of this heavenly food, He commanded them to continue to make present and real this Eucharistic sacrifice. "Do this in remembrance of me," Jesus instructed His Apostles. So whenever we celebrate Mass, we do so at Christ's command, and in His name. As we find recorded in the Scriptures, "For as often as you eat this bread and drink the cup, you proclaim the death of the Lord until he comes" (1 Corinthians 11:26).

But why would Jesus ask us to do something that sounds as strange as eating His Body and drinking His Blood? When you understand Jesus' Sacrifice on the Cross as the culmination of salvation history, the Eucharist begins to make perfect sense.

The Eucharist in Salvation History

St. Augustine said, "The New Testament lies hidden in the Old and the Old is unveiled in the New." The Eucharist is a mystery that involves the entire history of salvation. It is prefigured in the Old Testament, finds its origin in the Incarnation, its institution at the Last Supper, and its full revelation and significance in Christ's death and Resurrection. Aided by the Holy Spirit, these events comprise the bedrock from which we begin to understand the Holy Eucharist.

The Eucharist has deep and mysterious roots in the Old Testament, conveyed by events, archetypes, and symbols all guided by the hand of Divine Providence. The most significant of these is the Passover. The Passover was the principal Jewish feast of the Old Testament. It was instituted to commemorate the Jews' liberation from Egyptian slavery and the fulfillment of God's promise to Abraham that He would establish a people uniquely His. By the same covenant, this same people would eventually come into possession of the Promised Land. God's people were commanded to recall this saving event for all generations and to keep this feast day forever.

The Passover Lamb

To deliver His Chosen People from slavery, God sent a series of plagues to Egypt. The last of these was to kill every firstborn son throughout the land. God told the Israelites to sacrifice a lamb according to specific instructions and to apply its blood to the doorposts and lintels of their homes as a sign for God to pass over their homes and spare their firstborn. "The blood will be a sign for you on the houses where you are; and when I see the blood, I will pass over you" (Exodus 12:13). God also commanded the Israelites to eat the lamb: "They will consume its meat that same night, eating

it roasted with unleavened bread and bitter herbs" (Exodus 12:8-9). Finally, God also commanded the Israelites to remember this great act of His salvation by holding a yearly festival known as the Passover: "This day will be a day of remembrance for you, which your future generations will celebrate with pilgrimage to the LORD; you will celebrate it as a statute forever" (Exodus 12:14).

Many centuries later, it was precisely at the Passover meal when Jesus instituted a New and everlasting Covenant and gave His friends the greatest gift of all – His Body and His Blood.

The Last Supper and the Institution of the Eucharist

At the end of Jesus' public ministry, "the day of the feast of Unleavened Bread arrived, the day for sacrificing the Passover lamb" (Luke 22:7). Jesus gathered the Apostles in the Upper Room for the Last Supper and told them: "I have eagerly desired to eat this Passover with you before I suffer" (Luke 22:15). Christ prophesied His Passion, revealing that He is the lamb to be sacrificed for our salvation.

Jesus took a cup of wine, and after giving thanks He said, "Take this and share it among yourselves" (Luke 22:17). "Then he took the bread, said the blessing, broke it, and gave it to them, saying, 'This is my body, which will be given for you; do this in memory of me'" (Luke 22:19). Christ instituted the Eucharist and commanded that we eat His Flesh and drink His Blood, signaling His victory over death through His Resurrection.

After He broke and shared the bread, in a similar way He took the cup of wine and said: "This cup is the new covenant in my blood, which will be shed for you" (Luke 22:20). Jesus instituted the Eucharist at the Last Supper as the new and eternal sacrifice. It initiated His new and everlasting Blood Covenant with God's people. As the *Catechism* explains, "By celebrating the Last Supper with his apostles in the course of the Passover meal, Jesus gave the Jewish Passover its definitive meaning. Jesus' passing over to his father by his death and Resurrection, the new Passover, is anticipated in the Supper and celebrated in the Eucharist, which fulfills the Jewish Passover and anticipates the final Passover of the Church in the glory of the kingdom."

Thus, Jesus became for us our Passover Lamb. This gift would win for all mankind the promise of eternal salvation. The Old Testament Passover lamb, whose blood saved God's people, is replaced by the Lamb of God, Jesus; whose Blood is our eternal salvation. Jesus said, "He who eats my flesh and drinks my blood has eternal life, and I will raise him up at the last day" (John 6:54).

Jesus has become the Passover Lamb for all Christians. Using the Greek word *pascha* for the Hebrew word for Passover, St. Paul writes: "For our paschal lamb, Christ, has been sacrificed" (1 Corinthians 5:7). The Church transformed the Jewish Passover from a commemoration of God's freeing the Israelites from slavery to a celebration of Jesus Christ's death and Resurrection, and freeing of humanity from the slavery of sin and death. God's promise of redemption is available not just to one people, but to the entire world. In Him there is now one, complete sacrifice memorializing and sustaining our own deliverance from sinful captivity. Initiated on the eve of Calvary's dark desolation, the Eucharist instituted through the Last Supper is a mystery of joyful light.

THE EUCHARIST AND THE HOLY MASS

BACKGROUND READING

Have you ever wondered: What do people who have died and gone to Heaven do all day? The answer is simple: they worship God, singing endless hymns of praise. To someone unfamiliar with the Catholic worship service, called Holy Mass, it might sound odd to think that Heaven is one perpetual celebration of worship. But someone who understands what Mass is would have to ask, "Why would you want to do anything else?" The Mass is truly and literally Heaven on earth, the wonderful gift Jesus has given us so that we may be with Him in the flesh.

Since Christ first commanded the Apostles (the first priests) to celebrate Mass for all Christians at the Last Supper, ordained priests have invoked the Holy Spirit and pronounced the words of consecration, transforming bread and wine into the Body and Blood of Jesus Christ.

The Mass is celebrated in two main parts: the Liturgy of the Word and the Liturgy of the Eucharist. More information on these two parts of the Mass are in your children's activity books.

Transubstantiation

The change of the bread and wine into the Body and Blood of Jesus is called transubstantiation. The entire substances of the bread and wine change, although they appear the same as they did before the change. "By the consecration the transubstantiation of the bread and wine into the Body and Blood of Christ is brought about. Under the consecrated species of bread and wine Christ himself, living and glorious, is present in a true, real, and substantial manner: his Body and his Blood, with his soul and his divinity" (CCC 1413).

The Eucharist is the Body and Blood of Jesus Christ. *The Baltimore Catechism* explains one of the ways we know this: "Christ could not have used clearer, more explicit words than 'This is My body.' He did not say, 'This is a sign of My body' or 'This represents My body,' but, 'This is My body.' Catholics take Christ at His word because He is the omnipotent God. On His word they know that the Holy Eucharist is the body and blood of Christ."

What Are the Fruits of Holy Communion?

When we receive Holy Communion, we are united with Jesus Christ. Our souls are strengthened: we need the Eucharist in the same way our bodies need food. The Eucharist helps us avoid sin and strengthens our charity. The Eucharist separates us from sin: it forgives venial sin and helps us avoid mortal sin in the future. The Eucharist also helps us see the face of Jesus in the poor. The *Catechism* explains, "Participation in the Holy Sacrifice identifies us with Jesus' Heart, sustains our strength along the pilgrimage of this life, makes us long for eternal life, and unites us even now to the Church in heaven, the Blessed Virgin Mary, and all the saints" (CCC 1419).

Receiving the Eucharist also unites us with other Christians. The very Body of Christ, the Eucharist, strengthens and nourishes the Body of Christ—the Church—whose members are gathered in that Eucharistic celebration: the living on earth (the Church Militant), as well as the saints in Heaven (the Church Triumphant) and the souls in Purgatory (the Church Suffering).

How Do We Receive the Body of Christ?

Anytime you touch something extremely valuable, you do so with great care. When we receive Communion, we are receiving the Body and Blood of God Himself! Therefore, we must receive this precious gift in a way that treats the Blessed Sacrament worthily. For this reason, the Church requires us to fast for at least one hour before receiving Communion, except for water and medicine. We should also encourage our children to dress in appropriate attire for Mass as a sign of respect.

One can receive the Eucharist on the tongue (the ordinary way), a traditional sign of our humility before God and an acknowledgment that it is Christ who feeds us. It is also possible to receive Communion in one's hands (the optional way). If you do so, you should make sure your hands are clean and empty, placing your left hand flat over your right. Be sure to put the host in your mouth right away: do not wait until you return to your pew.

Who Can Receive the Eucharist?

Catholics in a state of grace can and should receive the Eucharist. Non-Catholics and Catholics who are in a state of mortal sin may not receive Communion. Some question this decision because they believe it excludes people and causes division among Christians. And the fact is that it does exclude people. But the truth is that when we receive Jesus Christ into our souls, our souls should be ready to give Him a good, pure home. Our souls must be in the state of grace to receive Him worthily. If we are in the state of mortal sin and receive the Eucharist, we commit sacrilege, treating a sacred object unworthily, as if we don't care. The Sacrament of Confession restores grace to the soul and purifies the soul for the Eucharist. (We will learn more about this Sacrament later this year.) For non-Catholics and others who do not believe that the Eucharist is the Lord, to take the Eucharist would be a lie. The *Catechism* and canon law provide for very limited circumstances in which, in case of "grave necessity," such as the danger of death, Sacraments may be administered to those who ask, "provided they manifest the Catholic faith and are properly disposed" (CIC 844 § 4).

Why Should We Receive Communion Often?

Catholics are required to receive Communion once a year, but the Church warmly invites us to receive it much more often: every week, even every day! Just as we need to eat and drink to maintain our physical strength, so we also need to receive the Eucharist for our spiritual strength.

When we eat food, our bodies receive the nourishment they need to maintain strength. When we eat the Eucharist, our souls receive the nourishment they need to maintain strength.

Frequent reception of the Eucharist, explains the *Catechism*, increases charity in our daily life and that charity allows us to root ourselves in Christ (CCC 1394). This means that we see things in a more loving, positive, and hopeful way—a way that leads us to be Christ in the world, as all Christians are called to do. Charity helps us practice the values of the Kingdom of God and to steer clear of choices that modern lifestyles of materialism promote. Frequent reception of the Eucharist helps us to avoid what leads us to sin.

THE SACRAMENTS OF HEALING

BACKGROUND READING

Jesus gave the Church seven Sacraments – Baptism, Confirmation, Eucharist, Penance and Reconciliation, Anointing of the Sick, Holy Orders, and Holy Matrimony. The Catholic Church identifies two of these, the Sacraments of Penance and Reconciliation and of the Anointing of the Sick, as the Sacraments of Healing (CCC 1421). These Sacraments address both forms of sickness and death that all people experience – physical and spiritual. Though we all experience them, neither was a part of God's original plan for us.

God's Original Plan

The very first passage of the *Catechism* teaches that "God, infinitely perfect and blessed in himself, in a plan of sheer goodness freely created man to make him share in his own blessed life" (CCC 1). God created us for incorruption – meaning that we were not meant to experience sickness or decay. And He made us in the image of His own eternity – meaning that were meant to live forever. God did not make death and does not delight in the death of the living. Death and sickness entered the world only through the devil's envy and man's sin (Wisdom 1:13; 2:23-24; 1 Corinthians 15:21; Romans 5:12). "As a result, the whole life of men, both individual and social, shows itself to be a struggle, and a dramatic one, between good and evil, between light and darkness" (CCC 1707).

God's Remedy

But Scripture also tells us that Jesus came into the world to destroy the works of the devil (1 John 3:8), to restore us to a full and abundant life (John 10:10), and to set us free from the bondage of sin (Romans 8:21; John 8:34-36). Thus, Jesus Christ, the Divine Physician, came to bring healing to both our bodies and our souls. When He walked this earth, Jesus showed tremendous compassion to those who were sick. "His compassion toward all who suffer goes so far that he identifies himself with them: 'I was sick and you visited me'" (CCC 1503). Jesus gave the two Sacraments of Healing – the Sacraments of Penance and Reconciliation and of the Anointing of the Sick – so that the Church could continue the work of restoration and healing until He comes again.

After Baptism, it is the Sacrament of Penance and Reconciliation that heals us from both spiritual sickness (by the forgiveness of venial sins) and spiritual death (by the forgiveness of mortal sins). Through it, our relationship with God is restored. Only God can forgive sins, and those to whom He has entrusted the power to do so, in His name. Thankfully, He has made this power readily available to us through His priests (CCC 986-987).

In the Anointing of the Sick we can receive healing for our physical illnesses (if that is what is best for our soul) and strength for our final journey to God. In addition to the anointing we can receive the Eucharist as Viaticum – "food for the journey." This can be a great spiritual help to us because, "as bodily nourishment restores lost strength, so the Eucharist strengthens our charity, which tends to be weakened in daily life" (CCC 1394). The reception of the Body and Blood of Christ, at the time of one's passing over to God the Father, is a great source of encouragement as we recall Jesus' words in the Gospel of John: "He who eats my flesh and drinks my blood has eternal life, and I will raise him up on the last day" (John 6:54).

God's Love and Compassion

Jesus' compassion and love for those who suffer has been the inspiration for Christians throughout the ages, and they have generously responded to the sick and the dying. One of the Corporal Works of Mercy is to visit the sick, and one of the Spiritual Works of Mercy is to comfort the sorrowing. Many saints have encouraged us to recognize that among the best ways we can help our friends, family, and loved ones is to invite them to the Sacrament of Penance and Reconciliation so that they can experience the same joy, freedom, and healing that we receive through it.

Our God is a God of deep love and unending mercy. He desires that not one of us be lost or far from Him. Through the Sacrament of Penance and Reconciliation He continually reaches out to us with His arms of pardon and peace. Nothing we have done is unforgivable or beyond His mercy. In the Sacrament of the Anointing of the Sick, He offers us healing, forgiveness, and grace for our final journey home.

"Thus, just as the sacraments of Baptism, Confirmation, and the Eucharist form a unity called 'the sacraments of Christian initiation,' so too it can be said that Penance, the Anointing of the Sick and the Eucharist as Viaticum constitute at the end of Christian life 'the sacraments that prepare for our heavenly homeland' or the sacraments that complete the earthly pilgrimage" (CCC 1525). From birth to death Christ comes to us in the power of His Sacraments. His grace is always sufficient for our lives – and for our everlasting life.

RESTORING OUR RELATIONSHIP WITH GOD

BACKGROUND READING

Do you sometimes feel as if you are at odds with everyone – even yourself?

Do you ever wish you could start over with a clean slate?

Would you like to have a more intimate relationship with God?

In the Sacrament of Penance and Reconciliation, God enables us to satisfy these longings, which is why the *Catechism* calls it a Sacrament of Healing (CCC1421). After Baptism it is this Sacrament that provides spiritual healing through the forgiveness of sins and the restoration of our relationship with God.

The Sacrament of Penance and Reconciliation

This Sacrament was instituted by Jesus as a gift of God's mercy. In the Sacrament of Penance and Reconciliation, we confess our sins to God (through the priest), and the priest assigns us a penance – usually prayers to say or a good deed to perform. To make a good confession, we must have contrition (or sorrow) for our sins, sincerely commit to work at not sinning again, and, as much as possible, avoid the circumstances that tempt us to sin. In turn, God, through His minister the priest, absolves us of our sins.

Jesus granted His Apostles the authority to hear and forgive sins when He said, "Whose sins you forgive are forgiven them, and whose sins you retain are retained" (John 20:23). Such a verbal confession is in keeping with the requirements of our human nature, as the *Catechism* explains: "Confession to a priest is an essential part of the sacrament of Penance…'for if the sick person is too ashamed to show his wound to the doctor, the medicine cannot heal what it does not know'" (CCC 1456).

The Fruits of Penance and Reconciliation

The Sacrament of Penance and Reconciliation is sometimes called the Sacrament of Joy because of the tremendous benefits it gives us. God's love is imparted to the sinner, who is restored to

His grace and strengthened to sin no more. The Sacrament brings about a "spiritual resurrection," restoring the dignity and blessings of the life of the children of God. The sinner gains an intimate friendship with God and is reconciled with the Church, repairing and restoring his relationships with others. The Sacrament reconciles the sinner with himself in his inmost being, enabling him to regain his true identity as a dearly loved child of God.

The Fight against Future Sin

The Sacrament of Penance and Reconciliation makes us spiritually stronger and enables us to avoid repeating the sins that we have confessed. Is it any wonder that the Church strongly recommends the confession of everyday faults (venial sins) and teaches that regular confession helps form our conscience, fights against evil tendencies, heals us through Christ, and enables us to progress in the spiritual life (CCC 1458)?

The Seal of Confession

"The Church declares that every priest who hears confessions is bound under severe penalties [excommunication] to keep absolute secrecy regarding the sins that his penitents have confessed to him" (CCC 1467). This secret is called the "sacramental seal" and cannot be violated under any circumstances.

In the letter to the Hebrews, we are told that Jesus is able to "sympathize with our weaknesses" because He was tempted in every way that we are, yet He did not sin. Therefore, we're told that we can "confidently approach the throne of grace to receive mercy and to find grace for timely help" (Hebrews 4:14-16). Confession, the Sacrament of Joy, is how we do this.

ANOINTING OF THE SICK

BACKGROUND READING

Jesus performed many healing miracles as signs that He was the promised Messiah and that the Kingdom of God was at hand. In Matthew's Gospel, He answered John the Baptist's disciples' question this way: "Are you the one who is to come, or should we look for another?" Jesus said to them in reply, "Go and tell John what you hear and see: the blind regain their sight, the lame walk, lepers are cleansed, the deaf hear, the dead are raised, and the poor have the good news proclaimed to them" (Matthew 11:3-5).

But Jesus came to accomplish an even greater healing than physical healing alone. This greater healing He announced was "a more radical healing: the victory over sin and death through his Passover. ...By his passion and death on the cross Christ has given a new meaning to suffering: it can henceforth configure us to him and unite us with his redemptive Passion" (CCC 1505).

Thus, our suffering now has a greater purpose. It is no longer something to be dreaded or feared because it now has redemptive value if we patiently endure it and join it with the suffering of Christ.

That is why St. Paul could say, "Now I rejoice in my sufferings for your sake" (Colossians 1:24).

Healing the Sick in Obedience to Christ

Jesus gave his twelve Apostles the authority to drive out evil spirits and to heal disease and illness and charged them to make this proclamation: "The kingdom of heaven is at hand. Cure the sick, raise the dead, cleanse lepers, drive out demons. Without cost you have received; without cost you are to give" (Matthew 10:7-8).

The Catechism of the Catholic Church describes how the Church continues this healing mission: "The Church has received this charge from the Lord and strives to carry it out by taking care of the sick as well as accompanying them with her prayer of intercession" (CCC 1509).

The Sacrament of Anointing

Anointing of the Sick is one of the seven Sacraments of the Church — all of which were instituted by Jesus. It is intended to strengthen those who suffer from illness (CCC 1511). As St. James put it:

> Is anyone among you sick? He should summon the presbyters of the church, and they should pray over him and anoint [him] with oil in the name of the Lord, and the prayer of faith will save the sick person, and the Lord will raise him up. If he has committed any sins, he will be forgiven. (James 5:14-15)

Who Can Receive It?

The Sacrament can be received by any baptized Catholic (who has reached the age of reason) who is either seriously ill or faces a serious operation, is elderly, or is in danger of death from sickness. It can be received more than once – even for the same illness, if that illness gets worse (canons 998, 1004, 1002-1007). The person receiving it does not have to be conscious at the time of reception.

How Is It Celebrated?

The Anointing can take place in the person's home, in a hospital, or in a church. It can be celebrated for an individual or a group (CCC 1517). It is best celebrated when it includes the Eucharist and after the reception of the Sacrament of Penance and Reconciliation. The celebration is based on the elements found in the letter of St. James: "The 'priests of the Church' – in silence – lay hands on the sick; they pray over them in the faith of the Church. ...They then anoint them with oil blessed, if possible, by the bishop" (CCC 1519).

The Sacrament is administered by either a bishop or a priest, using the following prayer: "Through this holy anointing may the Lord in his love and mercy help you with the grace of the Holy Spirit. May the Lord who frees you from sin save you and raise you up" (CCC 1513).

The Fruits of Anointing

Anointing of the Sick gives the grace of "strengthening, peace and courage to overcome the difficulties that go with the condition of serious illness or the frailty of old age" (CCC 1520) and strengthens against discouragement and fear. It unites sick persons with the Passion of Jesus Christ and consecrates their suffering for participation in the saving work of Christ. If the person is too sick to receive the Sacrament of Penance, his sins are forgiven in the anointing. The anointing heals sick persons physically if that is best for their soul (CCC 1532) and is a preparation for their final journey home.

Viaticum

The Church also offers the dying person the Eucharist as Viaticum – "food for the journey." This is in response to Jesus' promise that "whoever eats my flesh and drinks my blood has eternal life, and I will raise him on the last day" (John 6:54). It is called a celebration because, through it, Christ gives us all the grace necessary for us to join Him, the Father, and the Holy Spirit in the joy of eternal live. It is one of the greatest gifts of His mercy toward us.

HOLY ORDERS

BACKGROUND READING

Christ promised that He would never leave us or forsake us (Heb 13:5), and that He would not leave us as orphans (Jn 14:18). Have you ever wondered how He fulfills these promises now that He has ascended into Heaven? One way is through the Sacrament of Holy Orders. Jesus knows that we are both physical and spiritual beings, so in the Sacraments He addresses both the physical and spiritual aspects of our nature. Along those lines, in Holy Orders He approaches us in the person of the priest – a human being we can both see and hear.

The Priesthood of All Believers

The bible tells us that every baptized Christian shares in what is called the Common (or Universal) Priesthood of believers: "But you are 'a chosen race, a royal priesthood, a holy nation, a people of his [God's] own'" (1 Peter 2:9a).

Christ has given the laity the right and duty to participate in His priesthood through our active participation in the Mass, Confession, prayer, and almsgiving. This participation also includes the witness of our life as we practice both self-denial and charity. In order to fulfill this mission

we need the graces of the Sacraments and the teachings of the Church, which is where Holy Orders comes in.

Holy Orders

Christ calls some men to teach, strengthen, and guide his children (the Church) by providing the Sacraments and performing particular types of service in His place. The Sacrament of Holy Orders is the Sacrament in which those men are consecrated in Christ's name to continue the mission that was "entrusted by Christ to his apostles … until the end of time" (CCC 1536). It is also known as: the Sacrament of the Ministerial Priesthood, the Sacrament of Ordained Priesthood, the Sacrament of Apostolic Ministry, and as a Sacrament at the Service of Communion.

While the priesthood is a great and necessary gift to the Church, it does not mean that the ordained minister is free from personal weaknesses or even from sin. But the Sacrament of Holy Orders does guarantee that the grace of the sacraments is valid and effective even when they are performed by a sinful minister. Why? Because it is truly Christ who is the minister of grace through the Sacraments.

Not only is it Christ who works through the ordained minister, but it is Christ who calls men to that ministry. *The Catechism of the Catholic Church* teaches: "No one has a right to receive the Sacrament of Holy Orders. Indeed no one claims this office for himself; he is called to it by God. ...Like every grace this sacrament can be received only as an unmerited gift" (1578). A call to the Sacrament of Holy Orders is a call to serve. The ministerial priesthood is at the service of the Common Priesthood of all believers in the Church.

The Three Degrees of the Sacrament

The three degrees of the Sacrament of Holy Orders are: bishops (the episcopate), priests (the presbyterate), and deacons (the diaconate). All three degrees are conferred by the same Sacrament of Holy Orders.

We can trace the unbroken line of apostolic succession through the bishops. The bishop, in the fullest sense possible, serves in the place of Christ as teacher, shepherd, and priest. Only the bishop can administer the Sacrament of Holy Orders, and he is normally the one who administers the Sacrament of Confirmation. The bishop has care over the particular Church given to him by the pope, and is "responsible with the other bishops for the apostolic mission of the Church" (CCC 1560). Only the pope can ordain a person to be a bishop.

In order to fulfil their mission across the many churches and institutions within a diocese, bishops ordain local priests to assist with some of their ministerial duties. "Priests can exercise their ministry only in dependence on the bishop and in communion with him" (CCC 1567). From their bishop they receive charge over a parish community or a particular ecclesial office.

The priest is the ordinary minister of the Sacraments other than Confirmation and Holy Orders. Because of his administration of the Sacraments the priestly office is sometimes referred to as the office of "sanctification" as distinguished from the bishop's office of teaching and governing.

At the third Degree of Holy Orders are the deacons who are ordained for a ministry of service. The deacon is ordained by his local bishop and is assigned his specific ministry of service by him. A deacon may serve at the celebration of the Sacraments, especially the Eucharist. He may also distribute Holy Communion, bless marriages, baptize, preside over funerals, proclaim the Gospel and preach, and dedicate himself to various charitable ministries.

A Gift from Christ

Christ's goal is for each of us to become fully mature and complete in Him so that we can enter into his joy. For this reason He has given His Church the gift of Holy Orders through which we receive the Sacraments, learn His teachings, and are shepherded (led and governed) by Him.

HOLY MATRIMONY

BACKGROUND READING

At the very beginning of creation God made it clear that marriage was a part of His original plan and that He is its author: "God created mankind in his image; in the image of God he created them; male and female he created them" (Gen 1:27).

God, who is love, created man and woman in His image for love. Thus, the God-given vocation of every human being is to love. And in a unique way man and woman were created for each other and called to become one in a covenant of love: "The Lord God said: 'It is not good for the man to be alone.' ... The Lord God then built the rib that he had taken from the man into a woman. When he brought her to the man, the man said: 'This one, at last, is bone of my bones and flesh of my flesh; This one shall be called "woman."' ... That is why a man leaves his father and mother and clings to his wife, and the two of them become one body" (Gen 2:18-24). This oneness becomes an image of the absolute and unfailing love that God has for us. After God created man and woman He said to them, "Be fertile and multiply; fill the earth and subdue it" (Gen 1:28).

From the very first chapters of Scripture we see that God created man and woman in His image and called them to love. He created them for each other and joined them together in a covenant of love (marriage) and oneness that cannot be broken. This covenant is to be "fruitful" and its work is to watch over creation and to partake in procreation.

Created for Joy

As the *Catechism* makes clear, God created marriage for the good of the spouses: "The acts in marriage by which the intimate ... union of the spouses takes place ... are noble and honorable; the truly human performance of these acts fosters the self-giving they signify and enriches the spouses in joy and gratitude. Sexuality is a source of joy and pleasure. ...The Creator himself ... established that in the [generative] function, spouses should experience pleasure and enjoyment of body and spirit" (CCC 2362).

God's creation was perfect and the union of man and woman in marriage was complete. Then came sin. Since original sin, marriage has been "threatened by discord, a spirit of domination, infidelity, jealousy, and conflicts that can escalate into hatred and separation" (CCC 1606). God's beautiful plan was soiled by the stain of sin and no longer worked as He had created it. To return to God's plan, man and woman need the help of God's grace. "Without his help man and woman cannot achieve the union of their lives for which God created them 'in the beginning'" (CCC 1608).

Jesus raised marriage to a Sacrament – Matrimony. This sacrament is a source of great grace for all baptized persons who receive it and is one of the ways God provides spouses with the graces necessary to live their marriage according to His original plan.

The Consent of Marriage

Although a marriage covenant must be witnessed to by an authorized Church authority, it is the exchange of consent between the couple that makes the marriage. For a marriage to be valid it must have the following elements: the couple must be free to marry (not already married, of opposite sexes, not close relatives etc.); they must freely consent to the marriage and not be under constraint; in consenting to marry, they must have the intention to marry for life, be faithful to one another, and be open to children; and their consent must be given in the presence of two witnesses and before a properly authorized Church minister. The consent consists of the act of the couple giving themselves to one another as expressed in the words of the marriage vows: "I take you to be my wife" and "I take you to be my husband."

God's Call to Marriage

Marriage is a vocation which is not simply a personal preference or a state of life to be lived, but rather a call from God. Men and women are called to the vocation of Matrimony for their joy and good and for the procreation and education of children.

The very nature of marriage where "they are no longer two, but one flesh" implies a unity and indissolubility (Mt 19:6). This mutual self-giving is strengthened by the grace of the Sacrament of Matrimony and deepened by the couple's life of common faith and the Eucharist. The Church teaches that "Children are the supreme gift of marriage and contribute greatly to the good of the parents themselves" (Documents of Vatican II, G.S. 50). We, as parents, should tremble as we pray and help our children discern the call of God in their lives. May all the graces necessary to fulfill this solemn obligation be ours in Jesus Christ.